WHAT READERS ARE SAYING

Ani Naqvi has given us a very special gift with her heart-opening telling of the closest call one could imagine, having just-barely survived of one of the biggest and most tragic natural disasters in Earth's history. Our gift is found in her ability to share, with crisp clarity and searing insight, all that she has come to understand about ways in which each of us can bravely encounter and courageously survive our own life's most disastrous events. The story here is jaw-dropping, and the powerful tools offered can be life-altering. I urge you to read this book, and share it with a friend. You will both be glad that you did.

Blessings,

Neale Donald Walsch

Ani pours her heart and soul onto these pages as she shares the remarkable story of surviving the Sri Lankan Tsunami. More than that is the determination with which she has since gone on to craft her life around her mission after the wave truly saved her life. When massive setbacks are used as catalysts for healing- that is when someone's life work begins....and Ani is fully planted on her path to help others through her lived story. I hope this book inspires you to find your voice, courage and path too.

Kate Emmerson - Coach, mentor and author.

TSUNAMI
The Wave
THAT SAVED MY LIFE
AND CAN SAVE YOURS

ANI NAQVI

Red Penguin Books

Tsunami ~ The Wave that Saved my Life, and Can Save Yours

Copyright © 2024 by Ani Naqvi

All rights reserved.

Published by Red Penguin Books

Bellerose Village, New York

Library of Congress Control Number: 2024923566

ISBN

Print 978-1-63777-668-1 | 978-1-63777-669-8

Digital 978-1-63777-667-4

No part of this book may be reproduced in any form or by any electronic or mechanical means, including information storage and retrieval systems, without written permission from the author, except for the use of brief quotations in a book review.

I dedicate this book to my husband, Andrea Barra, whose unwavering support and unconditional love showed me what true love really looked like and without whose support I may not be here today. My first spiritual teacher and guardian angel.

Contents

Foreword by Nate Berkus	ix
Introduction	xiii

Part I
The Wave

1. City Girl	3
2. It's Christmas 2004	7
3. In Paradise	9
4. The Night Before	13
5. The First Wave	24
6. Out of the Hut	32
7. A Small Respite	36
8. Higher Ground	49
9. Paradise Lost	52
10. Survival - Emotions Bubbled Over	66
11. No Food, No Water	81
12. We Start Documenting	94
13. Threats of Another Wave	105
14. The Long Night Out on The Hill - A Review of the Survivors	116
15. Dreams and Horrors	121
16. Day 2: A Waiting Game	126
17. Rescued	130
18. Ampara	139
19. The Long Journey Back to Colombo	150
20. Rag Tails and Cocktails	155
21. Day 3: A Shopping Spree in Colombo	164
22. Reality Strikes	167
23. Documents and Papers	170
24. Bags of Money	175
25. Day 4: New Year's Eve and a Hasty Retreat	182

26. Home	194
27. London Adjustment	197
28. The Oprah Show Calls	202
29. A Downward Spiral	217
30. Bell's Palsy Strikes	222

Part II
Picking Up The Pieces

31. Drawn to Danger	235
32. Finding Love	242
33. Celebration and Despair (Again)	253
34. Death Catches Me Up	256
35. Cancer Bites Hard	263
36. Remission? No Remission	269
37. I opt for surgery	273
38. A Decade Later and Stage 4	277

Part III
Healing - Universal Lessons for All

39. Lesson 1: How Our Thoughts Shape Our Reality	283
40. Lesson 2: Death is not the end, merely a transition to another dimension	288
41. Lesson 3: You have the power of mastering your mind	291
42. Lesson 4: We All Have a Greater Purpose	298
Epilogue	310
Acknowledgments	319
About the Author	321

Foreword by Nate Berkus

The pristine and remote beaches of Sri Lanka are among the loveliest in the world, and the local culture among the most welcoming and kindest as well. It was in this magical and distant setting that I was given the great gift of realizing who I am as a person.

I had always wondered how I would act in a crisis:

Would I be paralyzed by my own fear?

Would I be able to think clearly? Do I have what it takes to help myself, and more importantly, to reach out to those around me and care for their needs, as well? Isn't that, after all, the truest test of a person and their character?

Having been brought up in a sheltered, suburban environment in the United States, I had never had the chance to answer those questions.

Until December 24, 2004.

To say I was unprepared is a massive understatement.

Foreword by Nate Berkus

The Indian Ocean tsunami claimed the lives of hundreds of thousands of people, vacationers in search of a break from their daily lives and locals in several different countries going about their days.

It also killed the first love of my life, photographer Fernando Bengoechea, who disappeared into the sea. That day I felt his grip on me loosen for the last and final time in the churning, violent water.

He was never seen again, and I barely made it out with my own life.

There are several things that happened in the immediate aftermath of the tsunami. Perhaps the most important was the connections I made with my fellow survivors.

I depended on complete strangers for my survival, and one of those strangers was Ani Naqvi.

The friendship that formed in the terrifying and gruesome (my constant trips in and out of the makeshift morgue on a remote hilltop in Arugam Bay, Sri Lanka, being one) aftermath was born from a few key things about Ani's character, and – I know now – from my own ability to trust others at a time and in a place when I had absolutely no resources of my own.

Ani saved my life in many ways. Literally and figuratively. She took control of the injured and commandeered helicopters, her experience as a producer and her contacts made it possible to contact British government officials and the BBC world desk to help get us off of a remote peninsula where the force of the water had knocked out the bridge to the mainland, leaving a group of nearly 50 foreigners stranded, lacking food and

Foreword by Nate Berkus

fresh water, many of us injured and no one thinking clearly.

This book is not only the story of that day. It is a story about our humanity and the skills Ani tapped in herself and others to help not only me, but the entire ragtag group of shocked and grieving survivors on that hilltop.

Ani and I spent the next week together, being lifted by helicopter to a military hospital and then in a truck on the clogged roads on our way to the capital, and then with our small group of fellow survivors in her friend's apartment in Colombo.

When I look back on that time, and even the loss of Fernando, what I remember the most is not the horror and devastation, but the kindness of the Sri Lankan people, their divine hospitality and care for this anonymous foreigner coming to enjoy their beaches, and the magical resilience and resourcefulness of the author of the book you are about to read.

Tragedy changes all of us profoundly. I've heard it said that whatever demons you have carried can rise to the surface and force you to deal with them head on after you witness and live through severe trauma. I was lucky I had no such demons from my past to rise up and haunt me, but I watched as others' lives began to unravel around them in the aftermath.

I can tell you this for certain, grief and tragedy have a way of keeping us stuck in loss and desperation, and grieving and healing are a cyclical process, the course is not linear.

One never really knows when the feelings of loss and sadness will come, even all these years later. But there is

Foreword by Nate Berkus

another story within this one and that is the story of survival – physical and emotional.

To survive successfully is to allow the grief and loss and horror in, to face those things with the knowledge that somewhere inside you the will to live and, most importantly, to thrive – to laugh, create and share – resides.

∼ Nate Berkus

Introduction

In the pages that follow, you'll discover the life-saving lessons I learned from surviving an unimaginable disaster, and how they can help you overcome the personal "tsunamis" that inevitably arise in life.

Whether it's the sudden loss of a loved one, heartbreak, financial troubles, or a health crisis, we all face waves that threaten to pull us under. For me, it was the world's largest natural disaster of our lifetime, the 2004 Asian tsunami. And the lessons I've gained on that journey are now yours to benefit from.

Though you may never experience a literal tsunami, the principles of survival, resilience, and transformation I learned are universal. The waves you face in life can be just as devastating, so these lessons are designed to help you rise above them.

The key to peaceful change often eludes us. But in this book, particularly in Part Three and the Epilogue, I'll walk you through the steps that you, too, can use to help you navigate change with confidence and transform your life. Keep reading, and together, we'll rise above the waves.

In the end, I discuss how our basic psychology works, why you may feel like the world is stacked against you, and how you can use simple, yet powerful, tools to rewire your brain and start truly mastering life rather than being reactive to it. Read on, and you'll see how these insights can guide you.

PART I
The Wave

ONE

City Girl

It was the winter solstice, mid-December, and in London that meant the sun set by 4:00 p.m.

I sat at my office desk and typed my last words of a report due while the afternoon turned into a shadow over Big Ben, blanketing Westminster. Streetlights flickered on and the town glimmered.

It was dry outside for a change, a brief reprieve from the relentless patter of rain that had deluged London for days. Since I moved to my new home in Southfields, London, I lived so close to the Tube station I could run home in a minute, which was probably for the best as I always left my umbrella in the rush to get out the door.

I was done. I snapped my laptop closed, relief relaxing my shoulders as I stood up. I allowed a frisson of excitement to leak into me as I could start to enjoy whatever adventures lay ahead of me over the next few weeks. It was my last day in the office before heading off for my Christmas holidays. I could not get out of the cloying office soon enough and had to fight not to race to the door. So I went through the obligatory seasonal farewells. I turned to my colleagues and wished them a Merry Christmas. I wouldn't see them now until after the New Year.

I was glad to be out of there and sighed heavily as I headed down the busy streets full of shoppers to St. James Park Underground. I barely noticed the crush of commuters.

London felt dim. Even with all the Christmas lights on, the place was dark and oppressive.

I was young, in my prime, a recently turned 32-year-old hungry for success and ambitious, maybe even too ambitious. I wanted to conquer the world while at the same time saving it. I'd had such grandiose ideas as a child. When people would ask what you want to be, I'd reply, "A doctor, horseback policewoman, teacher, or social worker."

Not a lawyer. That was what my father wanted me to become. My father's family came from a long line of Barrister's or Vakeels as they were called in Urdu. The Vakeel tradition had been going on so long that my father was desperate for me to become one, too.

Being a doctor was ruled out early, as I was really squeamish. I had opted for journalism.

My father had dismissed my desire to become a journalist until the day I got a job at the BBC. Then he changed his tune.

"Oh, look, my daughter, she works at the BBC," he would proudly announce to all and sundry. He would tell anyone – friends, colleagues, relatives, even the man on the Tube next to him. The BBC was a world-renowned and respected news organisation, and his oldest daughter was a journalist at it.

But I'd left the BBC as a broadcast journalist five years back. I was now stuck in a no-man's land of contracting and finding what to do next.

Everything in London was a rush. No matter what time I woke up I always seemed to be racing against the clock. Getting to work on time, arriving home quickly, always in fifth gear I'd often think. Not that I had anyone to rush home to, but that's not the point. Who doesn't want to get home when they dislike their job? I felt stifled, stuck, directionless.

This had been a familiar feeling for several years now, a sense of general discontent and depression. Since I'd arrived back from Australia on my wild two-year adventure, a feeling of loneliness, heaviness, and despair hung around me like a black cloud. This feeling had been there way longer than just two years though. It had been there all my life on and off. A malaise.

I sighed heavily as I sat down. Was this all that life was about? Waking up in the dark, going to a boring job, making small talk about TV shows and the news at the water cooler, back home again in the dark, heating a microwave meal for one – and repeat? Surely there was more to life than going to school, college, university, getting a job, getting married, popping out a couple of kids, retiring then dying?

Happiness eluded me. Did anyone living in this city, so removed from the natural world, really feel alive? Were we all on a hamster wheel, no time to think, just going through the motions, fooling ourselves we were happy by partying at the weekends with friends and having momentary periods of escapism?

Finally, I tumbled into my flat and flipped on the lights. I had to pack and get ready to leave for my flight the next day.

Later that night, I lay tossing in bed, unable to sleep.

I had the strangest dream, first about dying in a plane crash and then in an earthquake. I woke up gasping, half awake and half asleep.

It had been so real I had to get up and listen to the sounds of the city to bring myself back into the room. I had to remind myself I was in London, about to head for the holiday of a lifetime in Sri Lanka.

TWO

It's Christmas 2004

Finally, my taxi arrived, and I was off. Heathrow Terminal 3 was bedlam as thousands of tired and pale Londoners headed off to visit family, friends or take a well-deserved break for Christmas somewhere warm and sunny. The place was packed, and check-in queues snaked out the door.

I was looking forward to spending Christmas away from London and with my best friend Sri.

Sri had been my first real friend and to this day is my oldest and one of my dearest friends. She's more like family, a soul sister. After my parents left me in London on my own when I was 19, I'd turned to my friends as family, and Sri was it. Sri was British, and half Sri Lankan. She had emigrated to Sri Lanka two years back and owned and ran a guest house on the beach.

I was single, and I'd spend this Christmas holidaying in paradise. The only slight change in the plan was that Sri was no longer single. She had met an Australian surfer in the spring. By autumn they'd already gotten engaged, and Sri had just told me she was pregnant!

Wayne had come on holiday and never left. Lucky Sri!

I was eager to spend time with Sri before the baby would change things forever.

I was planning more than a holiday. I'd arranged meetings after Christmas with some architects in Sri Lanka. I too was going to start the process of having a slice of paradise in the glistening, warm Indian ocean.

THREE

In Paradise

I walked out of the airport the next day in the capital city, Colombo. It was the complete opposite of dreary London. Bright sunshine, a myriad of colours, sights and sounds, all vying for my attention.

A cacophony of noise bombarded me. Hordes of taxis and rickshawallas surrounded me.

Finally, I saw my guy and got in the taxi, relieved. I promptly kicked off my boots to replace them with flip flops and immediately asked for the air con.

"Bamablipitya, please."

I was disorientated by my overnight flight and sleepy brain. The sun was so hot there was a haze over the city, and the humidity almost took your breath away. I began to sweat.

I gazed out of the windows as we headed off through the dusty streets, piled high with traffic, honking horns and beeping every second, chaotic like so many Asian cities. Here a horn was honked as a matter of course to inform others you were there as much as anything. It's the one noise that permeates every main road in Sri Lanka – the constant honking and hooting. Staying off the beaten track was preferable unless you liked to be woken up by the buses honking their horns at 4:00 a.m.

Cars and buses drove wildly, careening in front, rickshaws scraping past dangerously, manoeuvring themselves into the tiniest of gaps. Thambali stalls by the side of the road selling fresh king coconuts and street hawkers with lush tropical fruits. We drove past ramshackle buildings, makeshift huts with corrugated iron roofs, and toothless smiling, old ladies hanging their washing by the side of a busy road.

The buses were painted in bright colours – red, or blue and white – rusty with doors open and young, small, skinny boys hanging precariously half in and half out. Always staring at you as though you're another species.

We snaked through the traffic, winding in and out heading towards the city. I felt grubby, sticky, and dirty. I'd only been here for a few minutes, but the heat, dust, and a 12-hour flight had a way of doing that. No matter, in just a short while I'd be swimming in the pool at the Hilton with a cocktail in my hand. I smiled at the thought.

A Scottish friend of mine, Becky, was living in Sri Lanka and working for a big company. She had an apartment in the hustle and bustle of Colombo, and I was going to stay with her before heading to Arugam Bay to Sri and her new guesthouse. The plan was to dump my bags and meet her at the Hilton for a cocktail where she would join me after work.

I arrived at Becky's place and after a quick change, I headed out the door with a cursory glance behind. I couldn't wait to get in the cool pool and sip cocktails while watching the big, orange sunset with its pink and purple hues.

Another crazy rickshaw ride later I walked into the cool, air-conditioned lobby of the Hilton and made my way straight to the pool. Young men in white, pressed uniforms opened doors as I arrived, and I made my way to a sun lounger. The late afternoon sun caressed, its warmth filling me like an iceberg melting. There was something about Sri Lanka even though it was an assault on the senses that you instantly begin to relax; of course, being in a 5-star hotel helped.

I found my spot and ordered my favourite cocktail, a pina colada, tropical, sweet, refreshing, and long. Becky hadn't arrived yet, so I immediately jumped into the pool bathed in warm, bath-like water. Another thing I loved about being here is the water; it was always warm, lapping around, holding you in a warm embrace. You could spend hours in it, as it was the same as body temperature.

I lay on my back looking at the cityscape of buildings on the skyline against the burnt orange sun, so close and big, hanging low on the horizon. Being so close to the equator, the sun was very different to London, its colour was deeper, and it seemed much bigger.

Ribbons of dusky pinks, deep burnt oranges, coral, and peaches lay in the sky as the sun hung low just a mere metre or two above the pool as it started its trajectory down. Here the sunset was regular and fast, always between 6:00-7:00 p.m. not like the long-drawn-out summer days in London or the short days in winter. Always twelve hours of sun and twelve hours of dark.

Suddenly, I heard a voice behind me and Becky appeared. I smiled widely, turning to see her walking through the door out into the pool area, the sun behind obscuring her face.

We spent the evening catching up and eating and drinking. Eventually tired and jet lagged from the flight, we headed back to her apartment. The next day I was heading to Arugam Bay while she was off to Scotland to spend Christmas with her family.

FOUR

The Night Before

Sri had arranged a taxi to pick me up from the apartment on the 23 December and take me to Arugam Bay where her guest house, the Galaxy Lounge, was located. It was across the other side of the island of Sri Lanka, on the east coast, completely opposite to Colombo. It was the most popular place to surf in Sri Lanka and had a famous point break that many regarded as one of the best surf spots in the world.

Technically, it wasn't in season and was meant to be monsoon time; but this year, like many others, the weather was just perfect and offered up sunny days with no rain. I'd been sure to check the weather report way in advance so I didn't end up washed out in heavy rains when I craved the sun so much.

We were traveling far away from Colombo on the west coast, heading to the east coast of Sri Lanka.

The road to the east took us up to Ratnapura, the gem capital of Sri Lanka, famed for its precious blue and golden sapphires and we began to move through the middle of the island. As we drove past tea plantations, the cars lessened and the green, hilly countryside came into view. As we got closer to the coast, the roads became bumpy, full of potholes, and we were constantly jigging and jumping around. It's one of the most uncomfortable journeys you can do, but the payoff is seeing wild elephants by the side of the road, buffalo grazing, storks feeding, and a host of other wildlife as we drove into the relatively unspoilt and wilder east side.

I loved the wild remoteness of it all.

While I bounced around uncomfortably, I stopped to take pictures of groups of elephants in the brush in the distance and huge monitor lizards crossing the road.

Arugam Bay was truly a tiny place, with a population of a few thousand, and everything is dotted along a single road that parallels the coast.

Finally, we arrived. It was still daylight as we pulled into the sandy, dusty driveway, and a pack of straw haired dogs came running up to the car as I gingerly disembarked.

Galaxy Lounge really felt like paradise, far removed from the hustle of Colombo and even sleepier and quieter than the relative busyness of the south coast, which is where most of the tourists flocked.

Sri came running out from the restaurant as soon as we pulled up, a big beaming smile on her face.

"Ani, you're here!" she exclaimed, as she took me in her arms and we had a long and warm hug. "It's so good to see you."

"You, too, I can't believe you're preggers!" I shrieked. "How far are you, honestly?" I asked, eyeing her flat belly.

"Just past 12 weeks," she said.

"I'm so excited for you," I enthused, truly excited to see her and basked in her good news. Sri had always since I'd met her wanted to be a mum, and now *her* dream was coming true.

"But what am I going to do now you are coupled off and banged up?" I asked laughing.

"I know, it all happened so quickly," she replied.

"You must tell me everything! I want all the details." I crinkled my eyes at her in that knowing way that best girlfriends do with a glint in my eyes. "And I need to meet the man."

"Yes, yes, let's go to your room and I'll tell you all. But meet Wayne."

He was walking towards us.

Wayne was a 6 ft 5 Australian with shaggy blonde hair and broad shoulders.

I stood next to her as we talked to Wayne.

"You two truly do look like sisters," he said in his broad Australian drawl.

"Yes," I laughed. "It's just that I apparently come across as abrasive by people when they first meet me, but everyone loves Sri!"

Sri chuckled.

"Ani has what we term as her resting bitch face. Unless she is smiling, she looks surly and moody. But she is not really at all."

"It's just my face I tell people. I can't help it," I exclaimed.

"Well, I think you look like you need a drink and to get into the ocean," he said warmly. "I will leave you two to catch up."

Wayne had come to Arugam Bay that April and had been intending to go to Costa Rica straight after. He'd met Sri while staying at the Galaxy Lounge, and they'd promptly fallen in love.

A mere five months later on a trip back to London in October, they'd announced they were pregnant and engaged at the same time.

Sri and I looked similar. People often mistook us for sisters. Apart from our colouring, we shared a great smile and a habit of infectious laughter that was one of the mainstays of our friendship over the years.

Sri had long, thick, black hair with dark conker-coloured eyes. She also had a mischievous twinkle in them and a smattering of freckles on an oval face, with full, perfectly formed lips. Her face was often adorned with a beautiful smile that lit her up like an angel. In fact, her full name was Srianjali, which was fitting, as it meant great angel.

She was undeniably beautiful but also so warm and friendly that people were attracted to her like a bee is to honey. Everyone fell in love with her instantly.

I'd accompanied Sri here on her trip the year before when she'd gone looking for land to buy for a business to run while living here. The journey took us to the remote little surfing village where we were now standing. We'd arrived in the dark in heavy, warm rain, drops as large as golf balls in a steady and relentless downpour, the middle of monsoon season.

We didn't stay long, but long enough for her to know she'd found her piece of paradise.

First, she'd taken on a failing restaurant and guest house business with a local partner and had started rebuilding and refurbishing the place, bringing a warmth and love it had lacked before.

The place was close to the beach but also had a wide expanse of land that went quite far away from the beach. Desert-like in its appearance due to the sandy garden, with a mix of wooden cabanas made from kajan, palm tree branches, and fronds to give it a rustic feel.

She had built a couple of concrete huts, and an artist friend of hers painted beautiful murals on the side of the buildings, one depicting an underwater scene resplendent with sharks and aquatic life, another with frangipani flowers and other artistic musings.

I instantly fell in love with these new huts.

"Can I have one of the new concrete huts?" I asked.

"What? Don't you want a more rustic cabana, Ani? They are lighter and airier, and you can hear the ocean waves roaring along the shore."

"Yes, but they also have a tendency to have insects, squirrels, and chipmunks rustling through the roofs," I said. "I prefer something closed off to the outside world. You know how I battle to sleep."

This room was quieter and a respite from the noise. I planned to catch up on my sleep while here, so this would suit me better.

We deposited my luggage in the room, and she conspiratorially came in and asked if she could sneak a cigarette from me.

Even at three months pregnant, she had that instant rush of wanting a cigarette as soon as we were together. We always wanted to drink Jack Daniels and coke and smoke cigarettes as soon as we'd meet, the familiar association of partying through university together.

I laughed and she caught me up on all her news as we huddled together in my room, gossiping and giggling like a couple of schoolgirls.

We walked outside into the sun.

"Who else is here then, are you full?" I enquired.

It was their first Christmas fully open.

"Yeah, we are. It's Christmas tomorrow, so it's packed. We have one family arriving later, a family who are planning to move here permanently. They're British, his name is Duncan and I think he used to be a tabloid journalist, so you may know him. Then we have a family of nine Sri Lankans in the front hut on the beach."

"Nine!" I exclaimed.

"Yeah, there are three generations – a baby, children, parents, and grandparents."

"All in one hut?"

She nodded.

"We have huge beds. Because Wayne is so tall, we have installed 6 ft by 7 ft beds in most of the cabanas – turns out they can actually comfortably fit a small Sri Lankan family of four on them."

"He is huge," I giggled. We were like naughty schoolgirls together.

Sri Lankan people in general were much smaller than the Europeans, both in height and stature. She continued to show me around.

"And there's a group of three doctors in the other hut right on the beach."

"Then we've got a Swedish couple next door, Stefhan and Anneli." She leaned closer. "Although they look like they are on the verge of breaking up to be honest."

She pointed to them sitting outside.

Anneli was a petite, straw blonde and a similar age to me, with piercing blue eyes, shoulder length, fine, silky hair and an air of steely determination about her. She appeared quite authoritative, perhaps even a little scary, even though she was diminutive.

Stefhan had a mop of darker blonde hair with a tuft at the top and a light beard. He was quieter and appeared grounded and relaxed.

The configuration of the hotel was two kajan (palm frond) huts right on the beach leading back in parallel lines towards the back of the property. The restaurant was on the left side, a cool, open-air lounge with comfy cushions thrown on the brushed sunny faded yellow, concrete benches and tables.

My hut was about 50 metres from the beach behind the three doctors, and Sri and Wayne's hut was opposite mine.

Anneli and Stefhan's hut was next to mine, 3 metres to the left and a little farther from the ocean. There was another family opposite them and another row of huts behind once more.

"Hiya," I called to the Swedes. "I'm Ani. So, you're here for Christmas then?"

"Yes," they replied. "We've come from Stockholm. We're staying in Arugam Bay for a few days and then we are heading off to explore the rest of the island."

As I was standing chatting to Anneli, a family drove up – a British couple with their kids. He was a portly man with three younger children, two daughters and a son. His voice boomed loudly.

"Merry Christmas, Sri," he called out. "Have a good day?"

"That's Duncan, the tabloid photographer," Sri said. "They've just bought some land in the bay and are planning to settle here. Permanently."

She told me that he'd already been in touch with her in the past as she had been partially responsible for showing him around the area and putting him in touch with various bits of land that were for sale. He and his family had decided to come and stay at Galaxy until their place was ready to move in.

Now the guesthouse really was full.

The day passed with Christmas preparations, drinking, and board games.

Sri fed us a huge Christmas Eve dinner with roast chicken and some grilled BBQ fish, salads, roast potatoes, and veggies.

I woke up sleepily on Christmas Day after a long late night.

Sri and Wayne were busy serving customers. Anneli and Stefhan strolled into the restaurant and sat down next to me while we discussed our relative states of tiredness from staying up so late.

We were all suffering from the escapades of the night before, but that was OK as we had little to do as we were on holiday, and all we had to do was have fun and relax.

Cute babies played in the sand outside hut number 1, while the mothers watched on.

The Sri Lankan family didn't normally eat in the restaurant. By their standards the food there was expensive, even though the average dish was around $5. But by local standards that was a lot, as you could get rice and curry at a local kadhai for around Rs 100, which is less than 50 cents.

They had brought food with them I could see, probably some shorties. Shorties were the abbreviated name for short eats, which were a range of Sri Lankan pastries, usually savoury with a variety of spicy fillings, including fish, egg and vegetables.

I watched the baby playing with its huge, chocolate moon for eyes with a bit of black kohl under its eyes.

Sri came over while I was deep in my reverie, enquiring about my breakfast.

"How is the Sri Lankan breakfast?"

"Mmmm, really good, just what I needed after last night," I replied.

A group of us decided to head down to Siam View, another hotel in the bay, as they were having a Christmas party there. Sri decided to stay back to look after the other guests, so I headed there with the Swedish couple and some other friends to go and check it out and enjoy some more festive cheer.

The sea was churning a darker colour than normal as the weather wasn't perfect and it was, after all, monsoon season, but this didn't dampen my spirits. The temperature was soaring into the early 30s, and that was more than good enough.

Despite our hangovers from Christmas Eve, we kept going. It was Boxing Day the next day, and everything would be quiet, so we stayed up late on the night of the 25th. It started off slow and turned into a big party. The restaurant at Galaxy Lounge was packed with all the guests, and we laughed, caught up, chatted, drank, and sat around the big dining table; large plates of food appeared for sharing. Everyone was in the Christmas spirit.

We laughed till we cried as we chattered away; the atmosphere was electric, buzzing with energy, laughter, and song. Wayne was a dab hand at playing the guitar, and while he strummed, everyone was in high spirits courtesy of the local rum, arrack and ginger beers that were free flowing.

This is what tropical paradise island holidays are all about, I thought as I leaned back and looked at the stars. Music, singing, and merriment under the inky black night with a million stars shining brightly down on us.

I can't remember what time I clambered into bed, but it was in the wee hours of the morning, and I knew I'd want a good lie in the next day.

Little were we to know that our perfect paradise island holiday would soon turn into a living nightmare.

FIVE

The First Wave

I was asleep in my cool, dark hut sleeping off my Christmas hangover. I had put in my bright orange foam ear plugs to drown out the outside sounds. I had my eye mask on, and I was wearing just a long T shirt and loose baggy trousers; it was too hot and sticky for much more.

Beads of sweat slowly slid down the crease in my chest while lying on my side facing the wall away from the door.

In between the door and the bed was an arch shaped freestanding rattan shelf, chest high, that also doubled as my bedside table. I hadn't even unpacked and had just dumped most of my stuff. But my special stuff was on the shelf. There I had put my passport, the book I was reading, my precious collection of mini discs and my mini disc player, speakers and other sundry items I deemed necessary to have within arm's reach of lying down.

I heard shouting and loud noises outside my hut despite the thick concrete walls and ear plugs. It was a rude awakening.

My pounding head became stronger as I battled to wake. My mouth was dry and parched, my tongue thick and furry. I was in desperate need of water but couldn't summon the will to get it. Uncomfortably, I turned around facing the door, willing myself to go back into a deep sleep where I could continue to fend off the effects of the killer hangover I seem to have woken up with.

But the noise did not stop. I heard the loud English guy, Duncan, yelling and a muffled kerfuffle through my ear plugs. Why was it so noisy so early in the morning? I glanced at my watch. It wasn't even 8:30 a.m. yet!

"Shut up!" I groaned grumpily.

But instead of Duncan shutting up, the noises got louder, more voices were added to his, and now it sounded like there were a few people all shouting at the same time.

What on Earth was going on? Was Duncan having a row with someone? What could be causing the commotion at this early hour?

The next second there was a huge crashing sound and suddenly the heavy wooden door to my hut burst open, daylight pouring into the otherwise pitch-dark room. My room was flooded with the glare of the sun. I reached my arm up over in protection; my body flinched instinctively from whomever or whatever was responsible.

In the split second it took to do all of that, a surge of water flooded in.

My mind raced to search why this had happened. Maybe the full moon that day had caused a larger than normal wave, a freak tidal wave? My hut was close to the beach — it was feasible the wave had breached the restaurant and flooded the closest huts.

A thousand thoughts penetrated my brain in milliseconds while I tried to compute what was going on.

OMG my passport! It was resting right next to the door, on the bottom shelf, along with my precious collection of mini discs that had taken years to assemble, and other favourite items as water submerged them under and began swirling them away, out of reach and sight.

So many things happened all at once. I sat up, preparing to snatch my passport, but before I could move, I was hit by a dirty, inky black wall of angry, thundering water.

Now the water came in from the top of the door, tons of it and so fast. It filled my room in an instant. My brain was battling to make sense of what was going on.

One moment I was asleep with a hangover and the next I was pushed down underwater as the weight of the ocean bombarded into my room.

I was in a wet, pitch-black hell.

All around me the water was pummeling me, swirling me around and around, attacking me and pushing me down to the ground. The force was so strong I was completely and utterly powerless. I surfaced and gasped for air.

I was swirling around in a soup of water with furniture smashing into me, every small thing in the room now a missile. The table bashed into my ribs and then another stick of furniture, winding me, I gasped out in pain and immediately started gulping dirty seawater in.

The bed was afloat, the contents of my suitcase and belongings tossed about, the desk and chair in the room upended and broken as the water smashed it, leaving legs of chairs and tables unattached to its top, relentlessly hitting into me.

The noise was deafening, I'd never heard anything like it. Where was it coming from? I could hear a roar so loud it felt as if it may burst my eardrums from the pressure and sound.

There was no respite from the pounding of water. Where the hell was the ceiling? I was blind with panic, no idea of what hell I was in, was I dreaming? Was this one of my nightmares?

My breath was fast and ragged, but I couldn't breathe properly, I was underwater, and while I gasped for air, all I got in return was huge gulps of water instead.

I was rolling around like a grain of rice in a washing machine. The light from the door had disappeared with the entrance of the ocean.

Where was the door? I had to get out. I was going to die here!

The taste of fear constricted my throat, salt water burnt my nose as it rushed up, feeling like it was going to explode my brain and stung my eyes, burning and blinding them simultaneously. The power of the water was like no other I'd ever experienced. I was like a rag doll, tossed and thrown, limp and helpless.

An animal survival instinct had kicked in.

My only job was to breathe.

Snatch one breath.

Then the next.

I was sucking in what I could get.

Every fibre of my being fought, thoughts disappeared, all that mattered was staying alive and getting the next breath in.

Pure animalistic, basic survival instincts.

No thoughts, but LIVE.

I thrashed and flailed. Desperate for air, but the force of the ocean was too powerful. There was nothing I could do, except fight, I fought like a lion, clawing, clinging for anything in desperate hope I was tumbling around and around powerless.

I gasped for breath once more, catching a snatch of air and another lot of filthy salt water. I couldn't see, a combination of being unable to open my eyes as well as the darkness in the small concrete beach hut.

The ear plugs made me even more disoriented as I tumbled around, the force of the water had stripped me of all my clothes and jewellery as my necklace was ripped from my neck, my toe rings torn off me, and now the water wanted my T-shirt too. The shirt was being dragged over my face and head rendering me naked and blind, at the same time disorienting me further.

I realised I was going to die in this dingy, dark hut in the middle of nowhere, and my only thought was I was going to die all on my own without having met the love of my life, getting married, or having kids. Ever since I was a child growing up in an Asian family, I had been told these were the things that mattered.

It didn't matter that I had a successful career, a home in London, and was financially independent. None of that was important in the throes of death. I was just a girl alone, miles from home, and I was going to die without ever having truly lived.

As I fought, the pointlessness of my life flashed before me, I'd done nothing meaningful or worthwhile in my life. All my hopes and dreams as a child were smashed to smithereens as life felt like it began to slip away. Without ever having been in love, never having found my purpose, and with no legacy to leave.

Why have you wasted so much time? I thought. In that dark death trap of a hut, it truly hit me that I didn't want to die. Despite years of being listless, depressed, and aimless. I wanted to live. Amongst the terror these thoughts rebounded as simultaneously scenes from my life flashed before my eyes.

The reality of a life spent without truly living, bouncing from one misery and tragedy to another, heaviness weighing me down sinking me into various states of depression. I'd been like this for many years, and here I was with the option of leaving staring me in the face.

A voice within me rose wild and strong — **you do not want to die**, it said. I fought tooth and nail for each breath and for life itself.

One breath.

One more breath.

But the odds were against me.

The hut had filled with water, and there was no way out.

In that moment, I regretted having opted for the concrete hut, I realised a wooden cabana would have leaked light so I could have at least known where to aim towards for air.

The hut was filled with water, and I finally managed to rise where I noticed a few inches of waterless space and tilted my head back for air. I was battered and bruise by all the debris in the room bashing into me, but none of it mattered.

One more breath.

One more breath.

After what seemed like an interminably long time but may have only been a few minutes, the entire hut began to disintegrate. Finally, shards of light began to leak in. I only noticed while under the darkness of being at the bottom of the ocean as a halo of sun just like an angel peeped in, which gave me the important opportunity to orient myself.

At first, it was a glimmer of light, and I struggled to turn myself the other way around as I realised I was upside down, then it was a broader beam as the wave tore away the roof piece by piece. Excruciatingly slowly, the walls and ceiling begin to disintegrate and wash away. Once a part of the roof, next, a window, I noticed the light up towards the right of me and attempted to head towards that, but I couldn't, the power and force of the ocean was too strong.

Miraculously the walls of the hut started to rip apart and the light from the sun shone brighter, providing the lifesaving compass I needed as I finally began to surface. Within moments the hut was gone, and I was out and into an even bigger rush of the raging ocean.

SIX

Out of the Hut

I gasped for breath, underwater once again, momentarily surfacing and getting a crucial breath of air in. As I glanced around, I saw that whatever this thing was, it was serious enough to have killed people as I spied dead bodies floating in the water next to me. I was going under and fighting to come up the entire time, being tossed around and caught in the massive force of water. Initially, I thought it had been a freak wave. But my eyes darted, scanning everything in sight. I realised it wasn't just me and my hut but something much bigger.

This must be some freak wave in Arugam Bay?

No time for thought. I was being washed inland with the water travelling fast, still being tossed around in the wave and the bright, morning sunlight hit me. I thought if I can get to Sri and Wayne's jeep parked in the car park we can climb in and outrun this thing.

Then I saw the jeep rolling around precariously close to me at what seemed like a million miles an hour as I gulped in diesel water.

Stay afloat. Stay afloat.

Breathe.

If I can just grab hold of something.

Anything.

Stay afloat. Stay afloat.

I frantically tried to grab hold of passing things, but it was pointless. I was no match for the ocean piling into the land at that speed, and my fingers slipped through everything, barely getting my fingertips to the passing reeds before rushing ahead. I was being swept along at around 50 mph.

I was struggling to keep my head up and take one breath after the next. But seeing the jeep tumbling next to me I realised the further danger I was in. It, too, was hurtling along at breakneck speed and could easily smash into me and render me unconscious.

I was moving as fast alongside it.

Finally, I surfaced once more for a gasp of much needed air. My eyes locked on a sight. Sri and Wayne were standing and balancing on a pole above the water, I tried to scream to them, but my voice fizzled out as it was no match for the thundering roar of the ocean. I was moving so fast they didn't see me. But relief that they were still alive coursed through me and for the first time a glimmer of hope. Thank God Sri was alive, my first thought had been for her and her unborn child, so this was a huge relief for me. It was short-lived as I was pulled under again.

There were more and more bodies floating next to me. Men, women wearing white, with long, dark, thick hair entangled in branches and debris, white foam around their mouths, eyes cold like fishes.

There they were right next to me, one man prone, arms out wide, lifeless and then another and another and another. I'd never seen a dead body before, and now I was seeing so many. White and brown skin. Old bodies and babies. Young men and women. Everyone.

I could see how some of the women had got tangled up by their hair. They had branches or even trees stuck to them. It must have pulled them down, drowning them. There their gorgeous thick luscious hair was a death sentence.

My mind was racing ... I was moving so fast and I knew I needed to stop somehow, but I was pulled under again once more.

Then I noticed the jungle about to start. I scanned the scene in milliseconds, my survival instincts immediately assessing the risk of death.

The trees of the jungle loomed ominously ahead, and I knew instinctively that if I continued a tree or some other debris would knock me out, and I'd become unconscious and drown like these poor other people. I could not get knocked unconscious. I had to stay awake.

Fear gripped me in its vice-like hand and as I was being washed inland, racing with the force of this water.

Suddenly, again I was under water. I'd become trapped as a falling building sucked me under with it. More falling debris landed on me pushing me deeper and deeper under.

I was pushed down to the bottom again blind with the darkness down there.

I was trapped, and I was upside down, again. And this time there was debris from a building trapping me down face first.

I'm done for, for sure this time, I helplessly thought. This was the second time I thought I was going to die, and this time I was sure I could not make it out. I was deep under water. When was this horror going to end? Trapped. Arms and legs scrabbling around, I began drowning again.

Suddenly, a memory came flooding back to me from the recesses of my mind.

Years ago, I had my palm read.

"You are going to have a near-death experience, but you will survive it," the palm reader had told me.

I had forgotten this over the years, but right then in that very moment the memory came back to me, and just as the thought popped back in my head, a voice deep within me, either my soul, or a guardian angel called to me and said, "This isn't your time, Ani. You will survive this."

Once that memory resurfaced in me, I felt some solace as I realised this was the near-death experience the palm reader had warned me of, and despite my thoughts that I was going to die, I would survive this. This buoyed me and a surge of hope shimmered.

SEVEN

A Small Respite

The tsunami's power shifted the debris off me, and I surfaced once more. Again I gulped in huge breaths of air.

At the same time, I caught a break and was thrown straight into the path of a tree that was still standing. On the impact, I was totally winded, but it was a lifeline and I grabbed for it and hung on desperately.

Even though I was still underwater, there'd be an occasional lull, which enabled me to surface for those crucial breaths that kept me alive.

Hang on. Hang on. Hang on, I kept telling myself.

My arms clung to the tree, solid and unwavering while water went over my head, rushed around me and tried to tear me away from it.

My arms were glued to the tree and fought the separation with every fibre of every muscle resisting the massive churning force of the ocean that wanted to pull me further inland.

Bodies were floating past me, so fast their lifeless eyes staring up at the early morning sun. I survived so far. I also knew Sri and Wayne were also OK. I needed to get to her and Wayne and hold on to the only thing or people I knew to get some sense of normalcy. A frame of reference I understood.

Had the baby survived this violent onslaught?

I held and held and held onto the tree.

I felt the force of the water slow. And then eventually the ocean started to subside as it began to be sucked back out to sea. The water levels were dropping, and finally I was chest high and out of the danger zone. Or so I thought.

I was bewildered, I had no idea of what had happened. Back then tsunamis were not really known about like they are now, and I was trying to piece together what had just gone wrong. I was in shock, my body bruised, battered, and bleeding, but I was still holding onto that tree for my life.

I heard voices now as the deafening roar of the water faded. Cries and screams. People calling out names.

Lucy?

Phil?

Mummy?

Distant, weak, desperate calls into the air with no answers against the eeriness of the aftermath of the wave now the air was relatively quiet.

I slowly inched my way out of the tree and turned to see other survivors in various states of injuries, frozen and shocked faces. They were all hobbling around in a daze. And most were searching for their loved ones.

I was too much in shock to compute anything other than my own reality.

As tears welled up, I pushed them down with only one thought in mind to get to Sri and Wayne. I was so lucky I had seen them safe and alive; I'd been lucky to spot them so soon.

It looked like the world had been turned upside down. All manner of broken things including barbed wire, broken glass, splintered wood, broken bricks, everything you can imagine lay smashed on the floor still covered by the ocean.

It was a beautiful, perfect day, the sun was shining, glorious, the sky blue without a cloud in the sky so why had the ocean decided to assault us like this, none of it made any sense. While above looked like paradise, all around me at eye level a scene of devastation and destruction dominated.

I began to half hobble, half swim back towards where I knew my friends were in the distance. I realised then that I had been washed inland a long way, I couldn't see the beach or Galaxy anymore. I'd estimate I was at least a kilometre if not three kilometres from where I had been fast asleep in that hut.

The floor was covered in an assortment of debris, so it made for a painful journey as my feet landed on broken glass or barbed wire ripping at my feet. The jagged edges of the whole world turned upside down and churned around.

I started to realise the extent of my injuries. I didn't want to look down. I knew I was bloody, bruised and every inch of me throbbed and stung, but still I hobbled towards them. The skin had been scraped off my legs, leaving them red, raw, and bloody. My face throbbed from where I'd been trapped under the debris of the falling building as it had also scraped the skin from one side of my face.

Shocked and disoriented, all I could think was that I needed to get to them, when I'd be with them everything would be OK, it would make everything better.

Single-minded, I set about my mission.

Then I saw them. Sri and Wayne were a few hundred metres from me.

I made my way gingerly to their distant figures. The receding water was now lapping at me waist high, and the destruction was becoming clear to see all around.

I couldn't see the floor as it was covered in the thick, muddy water. I attempted to swim but my arms were leaden, exhausted from holding on to the tree for so long. But I had to get there, to my friends, once there everything would be better, everything would be OK – the comfort of being with others would take the pain and shock away. I kept moving towards them step by step.

After an interminably long time I finally reached their spot, they didn't spot me at first and I called out.

"Sri," my voice was weak and barely audible.

"Sri," I tried again.

She turned around.

"Ani? Is that you? OMG you're alive! I was going to come and get you, but Wayne told me we didn't have time."

I started gasping with relief, as now I had found them.

"I almost didn't recognise you!" she exclaimed. "You're covered in mud."

"I am?"

I looked around me where some other people stood, looking dazed. We all looked like some swamp monsters coming out of the ocean. I reached up to feel my face. My hair was full of twigs, branches and mud caked my face and body from where I'd been dragged along the ocean floor by my hair backwards, my face was also muddied.

Sri looked relatively normal in comparison to me.

"What happened, Sri?" I sobbed.

"I don't know, Ani."

"But what was it?"

She shook her head.

"I was in the restaurant making breakfast when I saw something coming. Duncan screamed at us all to run. I ran straight outside and pulled Wayne from our hut. I was running towards you when the wave hit. Wayne was trying to pull me with him and towards the jeep. But we were too far and the next second the water swept us up."

My teeth were chattering and my body trembling, from the aftermath of the adrenaline on overdrive pumping through my system.

"Wayne," I called out weakly, Wayne was looking into the distance towards the shore. He was distant and shocked.

"I need to get to the first aid kit," he said in a monotone. It was only then I noticed that he had a big gaping hole that had torn through his left arm.

I turned away quickly from the sight, not able to even take it in. I almost fainted from the sight of it.

"We've got to go back to the hotel and get the first aid kit," he repeated as he turned on his heels in the direction of the shore, single-minded and with a mission of his own to focus on.

I was too dazed and confused to argue in my hysterical state, just glad I had found my friends and wasn't alone.

Sri grabbed him by the other arm.

"There is no Galaxy left, Wayne, there is no first aid kit," Sri seemed the most composed out of the lot of us, less shocked in my eyes, while I crumbled inside. I held on to her strength to get me through.

Wayne ignored Sri and took no heed and just kept saying again and again, "We need to go to Galaxy, we need first aid."

He started off in the direction back towards the beach, and we followed suit like sheep, too spent, exhausted, and traumatised to do anything else.

We started the journey back to shore, to find the smashed Galaxy Guest House and the first aid box that didn't exist.

"Wayne, there is no Galaxy, I don't think we should go that way," Sri pleaded with Wayne every step. But he was vacant and in shock.

"We have to get the first aid kit."

Unable to convince him to stop, we followed him down.

A few minutes passed, we'd been washed in a fair way inland with the ocean and the water had subsided. Bodies were floating all around us.

It was then I realised I was half naked, with only a T-shirt on.

In the recesses of my mind, I listlessly thought what the locals would make of me in my state of undress and being on the Muslim side of the island where nudity was frowned upon.

As we moved, all around us lay bodies strewn like dolls. Broken, in awkward positions, that same white foam around their mouths, eyes open, glassy, staring.

Once again, another layer of shock descended and the realisation that it wasn't just a couple of people that had been affected hit me; there were dozens of bodies.

This must have been bigger than I thought, but I still thought it was exclusive to Arugam Bay, a freak full moon wave.

The water had begun to subside and got sucked out to sea again. Little did we know this was another portent of doom.

As we cut a path back to the shoreline, I spotted my suitcase, upside down, half broken and started towards it. I broke off from the two of them as I made my way to my suitcase.

"Ani, stop," Sri called to me. I ignored her as I had to get my suitcase.

"Ani!" she called, louder, more panicked as I went farther from them. "What are you doing?"

"It's my suitcase, I have to get my suitcase."

"It's broken, Ani, leave it."

"But it's not mine, I borrowed it from Jo." Jo was my flatmate and she'd lent me her suitcase for my holiday. I had to bring her suitcase back. It just wasn't good form to borrow something and not return it, I thought obsessively.

"I really don't think she'll mind, Ani," Sri pressed on. "Just leave it. You can't carry that with you all the way." I looked at her, looked at the suitcase; it was one of the few things I recognised on the landscape that otherwise had nothing familiar there to hold on to.

I needed to get that suitcase. It seemed like it was life itself, a reminder of home, normalcy, my life before, not this horror show we seemed to be in.

"But I need to get it," I once again repeated.

"Ani!" Sri's voice was stern, authoritative, like a parent to a child. "Come on, we don't have time for this."

I realised she was right, I wouldn't be able to carry it in my state, my arms were leaden, and maybe Jo would be fine about it. I hadn't done it on purpose after all. Maybe she'd understand?

It's strange to reflect on how attached to possessions I was. When you're suffering from shock, the urge to grasp on to any sense of familiarity in the shape of luggage or a shoe overrides common sense. My main concern about the suitcase had been about upsetting my flatmate, and I forlornly left it behind.

The next second I spotted one of my shoes, a brown trainer. I headed over.

"Ani!"

I ignored Sri's call.

"Where are you going?"

"My shoe is over there," I pointed to an overturned brown trainer in the distance amongst the rubble.

"Leave it, you don't need it!" Sri called out.

"I can wear it, and it will protect my foot."

"You can't walk around with one shoe on."

I hesitated again as I forlornly looked at it in the distance and once again re-joined them, upset I couldn't get my shoe.

It was bizarre to see the contents of people's lives and homes strewn around, smashed, upended, broken, so much devastation and destruction.

The floor was littered with jagged bits of shattered glass, shredded chicken wire, upended fences with sharp pointy bits, the remnants of destroyed buildings, with rubble, smashed and spikey poles, nails jutting out precariously. It went a foot or two high off the floor making our journey slow with our injuries.

We didn't speak, we just walked slowly, picking our way through the damage. Fear, adrenaline, and shock had made us mute.

The thundering noise disappeared with the ocean when it was sucked back out to sea, and now there was an eerie quietness in the air, with the discordant call of names, and the crunching of people wandering around lost looking for loved ones.

We headed towards a raging river and came across Bari, Sri's business partner.

"Sri," he called.

"Bari!" she sobbed. "Oh my God, are you OK?"

"Yes, I'm fine but I don't know if my family is. I must get back to check on them."

Bari was making his way back the same way we were but was stuck at this makeshift river that had formed with the tsunami. We were still far from the shore, around a kilometre perhaps.

"I'll help you get across," Wayne called out over the noise of the river. And he entered the river gingerly to see how high it was. It came up to Wayne's chest as he waded into the middle.

"Come, Bari," he reached out his arm to assist Bari across and Bari jumped in doggy-paddling his way through. We watched in horror as the sight of them both entering this fast-flowing sludge of water wondering if they would both get washed away again.

But Bari made it across safely with Wayne's assistance.

"Sri, come on; I'll help you across," Wayne shouted out.

"I'm not getting in there, Wayne; there is no Galaxy. Come back, there's nothing left there."

Suddenly, we heard some shouting in the distance, as screams from closer to the shore began to reverberate.

"Tani, Tani, Tani, Water, water, water!"

People screamed. I looked up from the ground, which I'd been staring at while navigating my way around the debris, when in horror we saw what looked like another surge of water coming from far out at sea. As I watched, I saw it was coming fast, building, getting bigger and bigger.

"Run!" I screamed.

"Run!"

"Run!"

People called out to us as they ran past in the opposite direction.

"Another wave!"

Horrified, we watched and saw enough to know we had to turn around and run again. I don't know how or where we got the strength from as we were spent, exhausted, half dead, and again running, this time running for our lives. But the human capacity for survival is strong, adrenaline kicked in, and a sudden burst of energy propelled us forward. Meanwhile, I was frantically searching around for something to climb to get to higher ground otherwise I'd be under again, and I had to avoid that at all costs.

As we ran into the jungle, I wondered if the trees would slow the water down, I turned my head to look behind me. That was a big mistake. I saw the ocean had breached land again and that people behind me who were running were submerged once the wave caught up. Panic propelled me faster, as fast as I could with my injuries. It's amazing what adrenaline does, allowing your physical pain to be temporarily numbed while you throw all your resources into outrunning a second tsunami. Survival instinct doing everything possible to keep you alive.

Some local people appeared from nowhere, joining us in the run. Sri, Wayne, Bari and I were all running together.

"This way, this way," the locals shouted, and we followed them, not knowing which way to go — just in the opposite direction to the wave a few metres back rolling back in.

Suddenly, a small mound appeared out of nowhere and we scrambled as fast as we could to the top. We tumbled into a small clearing and stared wide-eyed, frantic, at the scene unfolding just a few metres below us. There were the four of us huddled there, two local villagers, and a German man who was frantic having lost his fiancé.

The second wave had hit, and it had picked up pace. People were running and going under. They looked like ants from our vantage point.

"Hey, someone's got my surfboard," Wayne shouted out, and sure enough we saw what looked like Stefhan, the Swede from the hut next to me, holding onto it for his life. He was being swept along in the wave on Wayne's bright, canary yellow surfboard.

As we stood there, we knew we were watching a massacre. One by one, we saw people disappear under the water as the water swept over them, and soon the land below was filled with the glassy sea. I couldn't believe what I was seeing, more people being taken by the sea. More horror, death, and devastation. When would this nightmare end?

As I looked around me, I noticed a few other people in the same place. Next to me the German man was standing. His face was gaunt and agonised.

"Are you OK?" I asked him gingerly, his face stunning me out of my shock momentarily.

"My fiancé, my fiancé, she was with me, but then the water came, I let her hand go, and then she wasn't there anymore. I couldn't hold her anymore, I tried but her hand just slipped away."

I stared at his frozen face, and the look of his pain was indelibly etched into my eyes forever.

"She might still be alive; you don't know she's gone. There are lots of people still coming up," I countered weakly but hopefully, but the horror on his face was too much to bear and I turned away, eyes wet with tears.

EIGHT

Higher Ground

We all realised there was no going back. From our vantage point now, we could see that every single building was flattened; there was no chance that Galaxy was there anymore.

For miles and miles around there was a scene of total Armageddon.

Exhausted and spent – we knew we had to head inland. It was the only thing we could do and slowly began our way to higher ground.

People wandered like zombies in a living dead movie, dazed and stunned, with various degrees of injuries calling out names of their loved ones.

"Louise!"

"Lucy!"

"Will!"

"Daddy?"

All around us haunted voices called out names of missing family members.

We passed a dead body on the way, a woman at a rag doll angle with white foam around her mouth.

I called out to Sri.

"We have to give her first aid!"

"She's dead, Ani," she replied listlessly.

"Maybe she's not, maybe we can revive her?" I grasped at hope but there was none. "Can we do mouth to mouth?"

"Ani, she's already dead," I stared at Sri hopelessly, willing her to be wrong, but she was right. Unable to comprehend, we continued walking.

I didn't want to admit that all these people were dead.

"How are we alive? How did we survive when all these people died?" My voice was rising in hysteria, and Sri shot me a look. Wayne was deathly pale.

Husbands looked for wives, mums for children, calling their names and here I was, single, and of no use to anyone, without a family and survived. Why didn't it take me?

As we slowly and painfully hobbled along the road, we noticed Sri Lankan people coming out of their homes, seeing the state of the survivors. The villages were on higher ground, which we had now reached. Most were not near the beach, and it was more important for the locals to live near a main road, and it seems only the tourists that wanted to be so close to the beach.

A Sri Lankan lady came up to me unclipping a sarong from her washing line, noticing my nakedness, and kindly offered it to me. I gratefully tied it around my waist. I looked at her blankly, staring straight through her shock overcoming me and continued walking, dead inside.

NINE

Paradise Lost

The morning sun beat down fiercely as we heaved ourselves to higher ground and entered a small clearing with a small village dotted around. We spotted a tree and walked over and sat down on the floor under shade. Sri was wincing in pain, and I could see her holding her side.

"Are you hurt?" I asked her. "It is the baby?"

She shook her head.

"I don't think so. I curled up into a protective ball around my stomach to protect my baby. But I think I may have hurt my sides and even cracked or broken a rib."

I put my hand on her leg, concerned.

"Sri, is this real? Are we dreaming?" I was unable to comprehend what had happened. This was what the end of the world looked like, here on this piece of paradise was where disaster struck, so discordant with the beauty of the sky and the sun.

"Yes, Ani, it's real."

"Are you sure?"

"Yes."

"Pinch me."

Sri pinched me on the arm.

I had felt it but was still disbelieving and willing it to be something else. I repeated this a number of times, until Sri replied again.

"It's real, Ani. It's not a dream."

Suddenly, sitting there I finally broke down. Knees hugged into my chest, head bent, I was rocking backwards and forwards and now I was hysterically crying, hyperventilating.

I choked, unable to take a breath through the sobs and shaking of my body. I gasped for air as panic overcame me.

My breath ragged and my body shaking uncontrollably, the whole morning I'd had no control over anything, and for someone who was a bit of a control freak, the whole thing was terrifying.

Sri kept her hand on my leg.

Next to her Wayne was standing. His face was stony with shock, and his entire body was shaking. Sri was soothing him, but I could see her distress.

We heard choppers in the distance when Sri turned to me.

"Ani, I have to take Wayne to the chopper; his wound is bad, and he needs urgent medical help." The ringing noise in my ears wouldn't stop as I stared at Sri blankly, sobbing and shaking in tandem.

"Don't leave me."

"I'm going to leave you with this nice man," Sri turned to a man sitting next to me.

"Can you look after her? I must take him to the helicopter." The man smiled kindly.

I was still hysterical and crying uncontrollably, but the next moment they left and suddenly I was without my friends, abandoned, hysterical and shocked. I continued to rock back and forth but now I'd been deserted by the only people I knew and something inside me snapped.

Through the ringing in my ears I once again heard the voices calling people's names, their voices hollow, desperate, and full of fear. "Donna, Steve, Mark," they called desperately for their loved ones. A voice inside came to me and said, "Ani, you're OK, your friends are OK, people need you."

I realised that I was alive and there were dozens of people in a much worse state than me, alone, with no one, injured, broken, looking for missing family members. Children, loved ones, husbands, wives, all with the same haunted look on their faces, unbelieving, incredulous.

A few moments later when I heard those people and realised their plight, I snapped myself out of my hysteria.

"Get it together, Ani," a voice deep inside me called, the same voice that had reminded me of my palm reading. "You're fine, your friends are fine. You need to pull yourself together and be there for others."

I was no longer hysterical, on my own forced to fend for myself. I took a deep breath and stood up.

I gestured toward the nice man who had been kind to me to thank him and tentatively hobbled over to where I could hear the chopper coming.

I made it over to the clearing where more and more people were congregating. A chopper landed and some people were loaded into it, fully dressed with all their luggage.

"Who are they?" I asked a bystander.

A hollow face looked back at me.

"I heard that a government minister had been holidaying nearby, and the chopper had been sent to pick him and his family up."

I stared in befuddled amazement as they were primped and preened as though nothing had happened and being airlifted to safety. It took off leaving us in the devastation behind.

I watched our only sense of salvation fly away, another wave of despair descended on me, what were we to do now? How were we to get out of this hellhole? The urge to run away and escape in the aftermath of this devastating disaster was huge, every fibre of one's body screaming to get out to get some sense of normalcy. Seeing our only salvation head off into the distance left us alone and bereft on this tiny remote island so far from home.

The urge to run and get away was deeply ingrained in our survival DNA, but there was no way out.

As I turned to survey the scene, I spotted Sri over the other side of a group of people.

The next second I heard a voice call.

"Ani, Ani!"

It was Anneli. I had last seen her late the night before as she and Stefhan had left the party before me, heading into their hut next door. She grabbed me and we held onto each other tight. I looked up and behind her was Stefhan. When we had spotted Stefhan on Wayne's surfboard from the mound, he had looked like he'd been submerged underwater, so I hadn't known if he had survived or not.

Relief coursed through my veins from seeing some more familiar faces, we embraced. I held on to them each for dear life.

"You made it!" I cried.

We embraced like long lost friends, holding on to some semblance of normality and connection before the tsunami.

"How did you get out, what happened to you?"

"We were both standing in the bathroom getting ready for breakfast when suddenly water flooded in, before we knew it, we were under it."

I wanted to hear more, needed all the details. But a shout interrupted us.

"Anyone got medical training?"

A local doctor was on the hilltop walking around asking for someone who had medical training.

"I do" called out Anneli. "I have done a couple of years of medical training." She turned to me. "I nearly became a doctor."

She was the only one who stepped forward. The three Sri Lankan doctors staying at Galaxy hadn't emerged.

The doctor led her to a primitive clinic on the hilltop. Stefhan and I followed her there. He showed her around. There was only one big room. In the room there were some bandages and some Tylenol: just the basics. The doctor gave Anneli a medical box and then said, "I'll see you tomorrow."

Before we knew it he had walked out the door and disappeared. Where to was anyone's guess, but we thought he probably left to go to the closest large city to treat more injured people.

The only doctor had abandoned us. Would he be back? We wondered helplessly.

Anneli had a look of steely determination as she surveyed the scene. She kicked into first aid mode immediately and began to give us orders and began tending to people's injuries and administered first aid. Stefhan and I helped her, executing her barked orders. Her rational, determined resolve was an anchor in the chaos.

"Stefhan, bring the injured here."

"Ani, grab the bandages and any clean sheets you find."

She ordered with authority. Stefhan and I made ourselves busy, grateful for her instructions and for that first hour as it kept us busy and we felt useful.

Anneli didn't look like she ever fell apart. She certainly wasn't falling apart right now, and I needed her orderly, cool, efficient manner. The night before I had found her an interesting, intellectual woman also with a keen interest in politics, and we'd bonded over our mutual interest in politics, justice, and social welfare. It was showing its quality now.

My assessment of Stefhan was also right. He had an inner strength within him; he was quieter but also had a presence that made you feel safe, secure, steady. He was kind and exuded a calming strength. I had no idea where Sri was at that point, but I was part of a trio, and we would stick together.

We went from person to person, checking their injuries, triaging them as best we could. I made my way to a shocked Sri Lankan woman who was hyperventilating just like I had been a few minutes ago.

"Breathe slowly," I commanded her, while taking her hand in my hand, and started modeling what breathing slowly looked like, by taking deep breaths in. "Look, do like me," I repeated. But she was inconsolable. I turned to her family, "You have to tell her to breathe slowly."

The lady kept saying, "Thani, thani, thani," which meant "water" in the local language, the same words we'd heard as the second wave piled to shore. The words got louder and louder and she rocked back and forth hysterically.

"Thani —thani — thani!"

Her family looked at me with blank faces, unable to comprehend my words, and this despondently hammered home my sense of hopelessness. I was no real help at all. A few minutes later, unable to bear her distress anymore, feeling hopeless and useless, I left her with friends and family with instructions of what to do.

As I made my way to the next person, a young local woman who was crying, I attempted to clean her wounds. As I turned my face to her, her eyes widened in shock and horror. She pointed to my face.

"You hurt," she said.

I reached my hand up and felt my own face. Under my fingers I could feel raw flesh and blood. I hadn't felt the pain yet, but I did then.

Gingerly, I tried to assess the damage. It felt as if half of the skin was scraped off down one side of my entire face. It had happened when I'd been trapped under the building under the force of the water. I realised I was probably doing more harm than good tending to people in shock and then giving them another shock when they spotted the mangled side of my face.

Between this and finding the panicked local screams and wails disconcerting, I realised I didn't have the stomach to do what Anneli and Stefhan were doing, detached, efficient, stoic. I couldn't deal with the wails of the local population and hysteria and shock, as well as the array of injuries, open, bleeding wounds, cuts, grazes, broken limbs. It all became too much for me. I was too raw for all that emotion and so much death and despair. My heart was at breaking point, my mind a mess. Every person I administered first aid to was a further reminder of the trauma, and despondency. I was too empathetic, each wail, injury a painful reminder of the scale of the disaster and I backed away in horror. I stood against the wall and watched.

Anneli and Stefhan continued stoically, Stefhan picking up patients in his arms and bringing them to shelter or shade while Anneli patched them up as best she could with the limited supplies she had. Tirelessly and methodically, they worked, dealing with one person after another. Anneli was to be dubbed the Angel on the Hill later and it was indeed fitting praise for her efforts over the next 24 or more hours.

By now, several people had gathered as more and more bedraggled survivors made their way up to the clearing.

I found Sri once more who was taking shelter in the shade with Wayne.

The three of us, Sri, Wayne and I, then took shelter from the sun in someone's home, a local Sri Lankan who had invited us in to get away from the glare and beating of the midday sun. There had been no room for Wayne on the minister's chopper, and we mused that the politician's life and his family were more important at the time.

But this local villager took pity on us in our dishevelled and wounded states and had invited us in and offered us some rice, but except for Wayne, we couldn't eat.

Sri busied herself by trying to clean Wayne's wound with her dirty rags, and we took refuge there in the cool, hiding from the relentless sun and the horrific scenes outside.

None of us had any clue as to what time it was, or how long it had been since we were in the wave. Time and space distort and bend in a catastrophe. The laws of the universe as we know it are gone. It could have been seconds or minutes for all I know but it felt like lifetimes.

Each Sri Lankan house waited for news of loved ones. When it came, it was news that their fisherman husband or small children had been taken by the wave, and a cacophony of wailing would start.

Death was everywhere.

The Sri Lankan's response to grief was full and raw. The women fell on the floor beating down on the concrete while sending piercing screams and cries into the air. I could only stand and recoil from this raw and uncensored expression of grief. Their grief pierced any sense of normalcy I was grasping at in this very abnormal situation. It was a far cry from the subdued response to death with the British who were famed for their stiff upper lip. The wailing and the screaming were becoming too much to bear for me.

We heard another chopper land, so we went out to see what was going on.

"I am going to see if they can take Wayne," Sri said and rushed off. I made my way back to the clearing and saw someone that looked like a medic running around. I craned my neck to see if they were taking people off, but it was too far from where I was to see clearly. I headed over to the other side to get a better view, but my walking was slow.

Another sense of hopelessness overcame me as I realised we were stranded in this tiny place. There was no way in or out. We were literally in the middle of nowhere. The bridge had been destroyed in the fifth wave, which was the only way to connect to the mainland. So, we were stranded on a remote peninsula and very far from Colombo. I ached to leave, to get out of this hellhole, but for now I was stuck in this nightmare.

I found Annelli, still working on the hill. She looked exhausted and I pulled her aside to take a break. Sri found us there and the three of us gathered, Sri, Anneli and I, in the shade of a tree just outside the room that was becoming the makeshift morgue.

Lithe Sri Lankan men tirelessly went up and down the road to the sea. It was the same road we had been swept along in that wave of water. They came back diligently and quietly carrying dead bodies up each time and laying them outside the room for identification. The room was tiny, just 2 x 3, and it soon filled up so they soon started just lining them up outside. They had made a makeshift stretcher to carry the bodies on and sometimes the bodies would be piled together so as many people could be identified before they got dragged back out to sea again.

Not only were bodies coming, but lucky survivors were arriving every minute.

Tempers were frayed.

"There are so many people coming up from the lower ground." Anneli said. "I need to get back to the clinic, but we have no supplies."

"How's Wayne's arm," Anneli asked Sri.

"Wayne's gone. He's been taken by the chopper and been airlifted." Sri revealed.

I turned to her, surprised.

"What? He was on the chopper? He left you here on your own?"

"Yes."

"But what about you? Why didn't they take you?!"

"They said being pregnant wasn't an injury."

I was perplexed but Sri was being approached by some villagers she knew so we were distracted, and I turned to Anneli to vent my concern.

"I think they only had room for those badly injured, Ani. Sri seems fine, but Wayne is gravely wounded."

"Do you think Sri's fine?" I asked worriedly. "She's barely speaking. She's complaining of stomach pains, what if it's the baby?"

"I think if it were the baby maybe there would be some blood." Anneli tried to reassure me. "And she is just three months gone, the embryo is small and protected. It should be fine. She may have hurt some ribs. But we can't worry about that now."

Worry and responsibility took over, and I fretted about what to do as I busied myself helping Anneli who was cleaning people's wounds and dressing bloody heads. Stefhan was right behind her, matching her and supporting her.

They had apparently broken up the night before, but here they seemed to work in unison as a team, and I wondered if this disaster would bring them back together again.

Sri was standing next to Anneli, and I heard the murmurs of a conversation.

"She's very worried about you, Sri." I heard Anneli say.

"Oh, is she?" Sri replied.

"OK, I'll talk to her."

"Yeah, I think it's a good idea."

"Ani," Sri called.

"What's up, Sri? Are you OK? Are you in pain?"

"My ribs hurt but I'm OK. You do know that I'm OK, don't you?"

"Are you sure?"

"Yes, I'm fine."

"Well, obviously I'm worried about you, but if you say you're OK…," I trailed off.

She took my hand.

"You know, Ani, you and I have had a lot of experiences in our lives that have helped us prepare for this day."

"What do you mean?" I replied puzzled.

"Well, we've both had to overcome many challenges already, haven't we? From your childhood, and mine. I lost my dad so young, and you had to survive yours and his moods and tempers. We are strong. We are survivors, Ani."

I nodded, tears in my eyes.

"Well, this is just one more challenge we must overcome. It's not our first crazy rodeo, we can do this. We will do this."

She squeezed my hand.

"Ani, you can do this. You are going to be fine. We both are. We are alive."

I looked at her earnest brown eyes and felt what she was trying to tell me in those moments. We were made of strong stuff and could survive this. I was in awe of her clarity in a disaster and her strength.

TEN

Survival - Emotions Bubbled Over

Shock, trauma and tragedy affect people in many different ways, and I was watching all of it play out in that clearing. Every spectrum of human emotion was there.

You had no idea how you would react until the crap hit the fan and tested the theory. This explained the vast array of differing responses that people had in those crazy hours. I likened it to the book *Lord of the Flies*. Some people lost their minds and behaved like crazed animals, desperate to get out, others remained calm during adversity, entertaining lost children with straw sticks.

Mine was a fight response. I reacted by getting angry. Raging angry.

Anger was my best friend in those hours and had me in good stead. It helped me have the agency I needed and without it I'm not sure if I'd have thought of the things that ended up helping us.

The long and endless morning turned into lunchtime. It was a haze of fear, sobs, wounded people walking around and endless bodies being brought up the hill to be laid in a line near the clinic with the bare medical supplies.

Sometime later I noticed a four-wheel drive jeep pulling up to the area and parking up in the clearing. They seemed to have supplies from what I could see from where I was. And as I headed over to them I had one thought in mind. A jeep would have a radio, a radio would have the news, the news would tell us what the hell had happened here.

My journalistic instincts from when I worked as a BBC Broadcast Journalist five years before kicked in, and I knew we had to find out what had happened. Information, knowledge, and the application of that knowledge was power, and it was time to find out what the cause of our nightmare was.

As I approached, I noticed there were two people in the jeep. The man was tall, lanky, and fully dressed with a mobile phone and what seemed like a car full of supplies. He had a thick dark moustache and was with an Asian lady who seemed Southeast Asian to me. She was perfectly dressed, with big, black sunglasses adorning her oval-shaped face, a gold watch dangled from her small wrist. She looked like she came from a normal planet, while we all looked like we were extras out of the Michael Jackson thriller video.

My curiosity was even more piqued.

"Hey, where did you just come from?" I questioned, in my British accent.

"We're coming from Arugam Bay." I could tell from his accent he was Scandinavian.

"But how come you got out with your jeep?"

"We were staying on the other side of the bay, at the Tristar Hotel. We were about to leave this morning to fly home and were already packed, dressed, and ready to leave when the wave hit. But the wave didn't hit our hotel hard as we were closer to the surf point, we just had some minor flooding downstairs and in the restaurant. When the waters subsided all our cars were intact."

"How come?" I looked up at him eyes wide thinking how could the same wave have done so much damage at our end of the bay and left these people untouched?

"The surf point meant the wave had disbursed by the time it hit shore, so it was much smaller and had already broken up a lot."

What the hell!

My mind scanned over the lay of the bay. I had assumed that everyone had been in as much trouble as we. But that didn't seem to be the case. Galaxy Lounge had been on the opposite side of the bay to his hotel. It lay in the deep wide part of the beach next to the lagoon with all the crocodiles. The south side of the bay was where most of the surfers headed.

"It seems the surf point with its reef underneath managed to break the water's advance and slow it," he said.

"That was super lucky for you!" I exclaimed. I was happy for their fortune whilst simultaneously mad at why we had all been the unlucky ones.

"Yes, we were lucky, so we grabbed what we could to bring it here to help." He gestured towards the back where he had an ice box, some fruit, water and other bits.

My head throbbed from the rising midday heat and the pulse at my temples was jumping wildly as I processed this new information. My hangover was long gone, burned away in the instant that wave hit with the rush of adrenalin and terror. But still, I needed some respite from the beating sun and remembered my original mission.

"Can I sit in your jeep and listen to the radio to find out what happened? I can listen to the news bulletins?" It was posed as a question but it was really a mere courtesy as I was going to listen to the radio one way or another.

The pretty lady sitting in the jeep appeared into focus through the window.

"Oh, but I'm listening to music," she cried out.

I stared at her incredulously, looking from her to the Norwegian guy, simply just not computing what she just said. My pulse was throbbing by the side of my temple.

"You want to listen to music? Have you had a look around here? Do you realise you are sitting here in comfort in the middle of a disaster zone wanting to listen to music? While countless others are without their family members, and my friend who is three months pregnant is over there?" I pointed to Sri. "We don't even know if the baby is safe. Look around you, look at the devastation, look."

The village was a wasteland of wandering zombies. There were around 500 people now huddled together on this high land. Most of the people were local Sri Lankans, but scattered among them were the tourists who were the income for this small island. British, German, Swedish. It was the United Nations in that small village.

The woman in the jeep looked alarmed as though I had given her a rude awakening. Deep inside I wondered whether this was her version of shock, listening to music as a semblance of something normal, but I didn't have time to worry about someone who had managed to escape unscathed. There were people dying, families missing, and we needed to get help as soon as possible or more people would die. There had already been so much death I didn't want to see more, and here was this person unknowingly thwarting my efforts.

From the corner of my eye I spied a young, shirtless man staring at the scene, his eyes widening at the exchange. He looked like he was in his mid 30s, clearly a tourist. He was watching the scene unfold. He, too, was open-mouthed at the woman's response, and his gaze shifted to me upon my admonishment. I felt his encouragement as he surveyed the scene, and I felt him mentally set his stall by me, and, in that moment, decided he was on my side.

"I think it's more important that we find out what happened? Don't you think?" I looked at him for confirmation. He nodded his head vigorously, then looked at the tall, lanky Norwegian.

The man stepped back and opened the door.

"Of course, it's OK," he said, and I was granted access to the jeep and the revered radio.

Relief coursed through me.

I carefully hauled myself into the jeep and began turning the dial to find an English-speaking radio station. There was bound to be a news bulletin on the hour somewhere as I glanced at the dashboard to look at the clock. It was five to twelve according to the jeep's clock. Nearly midday. Our first time check of the day.

I knew already from others that the wave had hit us at around 8:40 a m., and so it was three and a half hours since our lives had changed forever. I started at the clock in disbelief. Was it possible? It felt like an eternity.

I started dialing the radio knob to find something suitable for the midday news. I called out frantically to anyone passing by. "I need a local person who can speak English and translate the news for me," I screamed out, panicked. I didn't want to miss the midday bulletin and could only find stations in the local language.

A young Sri Lankan man volunteered, "I can!" I breathed a sigh of relief as he came to the jeep and began listening to the radio and translated for me.

"Seems there's been some incident, they are not sure what yet but it has triggered a tsunami," he relayed to me. I waited for the next news bulletin at the half past the hour to get more detail, as the news was slow to come. I eventually found an English-speaking station and my ears pricked up.

At first, they were just announcing the songs and I began to despair if they would ever get to the news bulletin. Finally, I listened attentively, turning the volume dial up and shutting the door to drown out the cries of loved ones looking for family members.

The bulletin started with a story about a crime event.

"Oh, my word, it's not even the top news," I gasped.

But then the announcer changed tone.

"News just in. We are getting reports of an earthquake that has struck off the coast of the Indonesian island of Sumatra this morning at 7:59 a.m. local time. Reports are coming in that the earthquake has triggered a tsunami that has hit the town of Banda Ache where some casualties are being reported. The tsunami may have hit other countries, but we are not sure yet where. We will report back as we get more news."

Finally, the news report ended and the music came back on.

It wasn't till later in the day that reports started to give more detail about what had happened. And as I listened to the bulletins at 2:00 p.m and 2:30 p.m., the extent and scale of the disaster began to come through.

"This wasn't just our island," I said to the Norwegian man who had been visiting on a peacekeeping mission trying to get an agreement between the Tamils and Singhalese. "This was an Asia-wide event, and news reports will be filtering out around the world. I should tell my family that I am safe."

"Can I use your phone to call home?" I asked the Norwegian man, who had a satellite phone on him that was working. Remember that in 2004 it was before the mass mobile phone era. A few of us had mobiles, and even if we did, roaming was not available. Added to that, we were in a very remote area that wouldn't have had coverage and anyone with a phone who was in the wave lost it.

"Yes, sure," he replied, handing it to me.

I wanted to call my mom. I knew she and my dad were in Pakistan at the time preparing for my younger sister's wedding. She was due to have her nikah (the official marriage part) ceremony in Pakistan in the new year, which I was due to attend. I didn't know their numbers in Pakistan so I dialed my auntie's number in the States that I remembered by heart. It was where my mum had lived for years before moving into her own place in Houston, Texas, and was one of three numbers I remembered. At least leaving a message at my aunt's would get word to my mum at some point.

As I dialed the number, I wondered what to say. But it went straight to voicemail. I'd forgotten there were almost 12 hours between the USA and Sri Lanka, so it was nighttime there. They probably hadn't even heard the news yet.

As the voicemail kicked in, I left a short message.

"This is Ani, I'm calling from Sri Lanka. There has been a big tsunami here, but we are OK. I am alive, and Sri is alive. Please let mum know I'm OK. I'll be in touch later when I can." Then hung up.

I turned back to the man.

"It helps knowing what happened, otherwise it just felt like the end of the world without any meaning. But this is big. There has been some huge natural disaster and we are part of it. At least that puts things back into the realm of something tangible we could hold on to instead of where your reality slid off the edge of a cliff into the abyss of the unknown and darkness."

He nodded in agreement.

I jumped out of the truck shouting out to anyone around.

"Listen up. Listen up. I have news. There's been an earthquake in Indonesia and reports that there was a tsunami. That is what hit us. It was a tsunami. It's hit Indonesia and other Asian countries. They're not sure how many people have died yet, but a few hundred are being reported so far."

People began to gather round as they strained to hear my voice above the chaos and wailing until they were circling around the jeep.

I repeated myself and said the same thing again and again. Throughout the day I broadcasted the news regularly just like a reporter at the scene.

Comprehension that we weren't in this on our own dawned on people, which at least aided our understanding. I had a strange feeling of horror knowing that what we went through wasn't just limited to our bay but across the world in Asia. The crashing enormity of it didn't sink in for many months if not years later.

I turned back to the jeep as the bulletin switched back over back to a cheesy pop song.

The owners of the truck set out about making themselves useful as the Norwegian man got some pineapples out and began cutting them into big chunks.

My mind was racing. If this were an Asia-wide disaster, then it was possible priority would not be given to the east coast in the throes of the civil war. We could be stuck here for a while. I began to realise the enormity of our situation and decided we needed some food.

I queued up for the pineapple chunks that were being cut and distributed to the people that had already formed a line. I wasn't hungry; shock, pain, adrenaline meant my hunger had vanished, but I diligently waited my turn so I could give Sri something to eat. I was thinking about long-term survival already.

As the Norwegian handed me some fruit, the young shirtless man who I'd turned to earlier, approached me.

He was disheveled but was fit, toned and slim. He looked worse for wear but not as bad as I looked, I guessed.

"Hey, can I get some of that pineapple?" he asked quietly. He was clearly American.

I paused for a moment, hesitant, weighing up the pineapple for Sri vs. this young man who had so kindly asked for it. Was her need greater than his? She was pregnant after all, but then I spied that the Norwegian had more so I replied, "Yes, of course" and waited in line for the next piece of pineapple for Sri.

"Are you on your own?" I asked. I stopped halfway through my sentence. He was on his own now, but nobody came to an island alone.

"No. Yes." He hesitated. "I'm still looking for my boyfriend," his head swiveling around surveying the scene, eyes scanning faces trying to spot his loved one."He hasn't come up yet. I am waiting for him to find us."

"There are still so many people coming up," I offered, "you might still find him; many people are being reunited." I didn't want another person to have lost someone, especially one I connected with so quickly. It was too painful to bear.

He shook his head hopefully but sadly, as if knowing the truth deep inside already, but unwilling to let go of hope at the same time.

"What's your name?" I asked.

"Nate," he replied.

"I'm Ani."

I pulled him close and gave him a hug, as he looked like he needed it. I did, too, if I were honest. I was so lucky to have survived and with all my friends intact. Here were all these haunted faces calling out the names of their loved ones as one by one people disheveled and in various states of injury made their way up dazed, confused, traumatised and shocked.

"When did you last see him?"

"We were staying at the Stardust Hotel getting ready for breakfast in our hut. We were in the bathroom when suddenly the water hit and we were underwater instantly. The last time we were together we were being washed inland. We managed to hold onto a lamppost, but then there was this sudden surge. I've not been able to find him."

Stardust was the hotel right next to the Galaxy Lounge and on its other side was the lagoon where the crocodiles lived. The desperateness of it all began to depress me again, so I busied myself handing out the food. Nate stood with me.

"Why don't we sit down," I said and the two of us moved under a tree.

I was drawn to this friendly, warm, sensitive soul, lost and on his own in a strange country far away from home. Sri Lanka wasn't normally a destination of choice for an American. It was far, far away and when the Caribbean was just on their doorstep, as well as Hawaii. He couldn't be farther from home.

At least I had visited Sri Lanka before. I had Sri and I knew a few people in the Bay through my association with her. But he was all alone.

I felt the urge to take him under my wing, as well as have someone other than Sri and the Swedes in our small gang of survivors. Sri was preoccupied with her own worry about Wayne and the villagers she knew. The Swedes had each other and were busy running the field clinic.

As Nate ate on the pineapple, I turned to him."At the moment, they're saying it hit Indonesia, Sri Lanka, India, Thailand, and perhaps some other places. I think given how soon it is after, they're probably not sure of the extent of the damage; but if it's across Asia in this way, then I don't think we're going to get out of here for some time. Resources will be stretched across the region."

My journalistic brain was computing all the evidence.

"Traditionally, whenever a disaster strikes, news is slow to begin with. Then as more information starts to develop, the scope of disaster becomes clearer. I think this thing is bigger than we think. And there was me thinking we were the unlucky ones over here."

"How do you know all this?" Nate asked.

"I've been listening to the radio, but I used to work at the BBC in news. I know we needed to find out what happened to understand what's gone on."

I motioned to Nate, "I'm just going over here to give this fruit to my friend. Do you want to come?"

I made it to the front of the queue and grabbed some more fruit as I began to turn to where Sri was. As we walked towards her, another band of survivors was walking up the road. Nate broke away from me and ran to them.

"Fernando, Fernando!" he called out. He raced to scan the surroundings, hopeful of bumping into Fernando any minute.

"Fernando, Fernando? You here?"

I stood next to him quietly. Then I took his hand and led him behind me over to where Sri was sitting.

"Fernando is your partner?" I asked.

Nate nodded.

"What does he look like? Let me look out for him."

"He's Argentinian. He's got dark hair and he looks like me, to be honest."

Sri was sitting on a mat in the shade, in a seated foetal position, with a look of pain on her face. She silently took the piece of fruit and slowly sucked the juice out of it before popping it into her mouth. Her morning sickness was more of an all-day sickness, so she was testing whether it was going to make her gag, but the sweet, refreshing juiciness was a much-needed respite to her parched mouth.

"There's been an earthquake off the coast of Indonesia," I relayed to the new survivors who had started gathering around. "It has hit lots of different parts of Asia with a tsunami but mainly Indonesia near the epicentre. So, it's not just us," I offered bleakly, not sure whether to take solace from that or whether the enormity of it was even scarier.

I was repeating myself again and again, but everyone was hungry for news and information.

A hysterical woman with a bloody leg sat down next to me.

Another person wandered up from the devastation below and started talking loudly. She was getting more and more hysterical, her voice rising.

"There's been more waves, another two came while I was down there, it doesn't look like it's stopping!"

"More waves?" Nate asked.

"Yeah," I repeated. "It seems we had been in the first and nearly the second wave, but apparently there were another five more waves, making it a total of seven tsunamis."

We both looked stricken as we listened to the woman shouting.

"Nothing is left. It is flat as a pancake for miles inland as it has torn down everything standing."

Other voices were catching her panic and rising.

"We can't get out, we're trapped," called another panic-stricken voice. A small gathering of people was crowding around this person and I hobbled over.

"What do you mean trapped?" an older, middle-aged Frenchman called out.

"The bridge to the mainland has been destroyed," a Middle Eastern woman replied. "The fifth wave took out the bridge, there's no way out of here and back to the mainland!" Her voice was high and about to break with hysteria at the fact we were stranded.

Screams of panic chorused through the clearing.

"What do you mean we can't get out?"

"The bridge is destroyed."

ELEVEN

No Food, No Water

2:00 p.m. Day One.

The amazing thing that drew tourists and surfers to Arugam Bay was how truly remote it was. It was a tropical paradise, on an island. To get there you needed to drive hours from Colombo. On your approach to the bay you had to cross a bridge that went over a lagoon and jungle. This was famously where the crocodiles lived, and the jungle was full of snakes, leopards and elephants.

Now we were being told that the bridge, our only way out and back to civilization and help, was gone. If there was no more bridge it meant, we were an island on an island. Stranded on one of the furthest reaches of the teardrop island off the coast of India.

We were trapped and stranded in our own little piece of hell.

It was after midday and the sun was beating down and Sri Lanka's climate was hot and humid. It must have been around 33 degrees or more already. I was parched having gulped so much saltwater I realised we needed some supplies.

Clean water supplies were low and there was no food, hundreds of people were injured, some critically. What the hell were we going to do now?

The locals usually drank the local well water; however, that water was most likely now severely contaminated. Bottled water was in short supply as it was an extravagance most locals couldn't afford and we were in a small village.

People thronged around, aimlessly wandering. I frantically scoured my barely-there brain for possible escape plans and solutions. It's amazing how adrenaline and survival instincts can keep you functioning.

The day was relentless. Minute and after minute more and more bodies arrived on stretchers. Some were dead. Others were dying. Some were injured. The numbers were overwhelming.

Nate was looking at everybody. His cries didn't stop.

"Fernando?"

More and more limp, and lifeless bodies, limbs akimbo, many with the familiar white froth at the mouth were being carried up on red, orange and black brightly coloured straw mats and stretchers and being left in a line nearby. Many were locals. Others were clearly tourists.

One Sri Lankan man pulled on my arm as he motioned to me to look at them, especially the foreign ones, asking me, "You know? You know this person?"

I glanced over at the line of dead bodies and looked at the first one, dead lifeless eyes, bloated from the water, a white face and looked away again.

"No!" I snapped.

Why was I doing this? I was with the only people I really knew; did I really want to be the person identifying dead bodies all day long, their faces engraved on my memory forever? I began to pull away from him. No, this was too much; I'd leave the carrying of dead bodies and identifying them to other people with stronger constitutions than I.

I wandered over to Nate who had now taken up a permanent post at the makeshift morgue, scanning the faces of the departed souls.

"Fernando? Fernando?"

I stood next to him on a couple of occasions while he painstakingly moved the piece of cloth covering the face to check if his love's face lay there.

He did this for hours as the midday moved into late afternoon, circling the small area, moving down towards the road we'd all walked up, around to the jeep area, the clearing, and the makeshift morgue. It wasn't a large area and was relatively self-contained.

I don't know how he had the strength to keep looking at those faces. I'd had my fill to last me many lifetimes. From never seeing a dead body to then seeing dozens strewn around casually like broken rag dolls.

But if my loved one was missing; I too would probably be doing the same in the hope that there would at least be some sense of knowing.

As it was, I already had the dead faces I'd seen etched into my memory for an eternity. The Sri Lankan woman with white foam at her mouth, eyes staring wide, her hair tangled in debris, lying there lifeless. The men floating next to me were in a prone position during the tsunami. All dead.

The European man, tall, Caucasian features, wan as the life that had left him had paled him into a ghostly white form.

No, I didn't need more death in my head, and I began to back away from the rows and rows of corpses being placed there for identification and made my way out calling out to Nate to let him know I was heading out.

"I'm going to go back out there, Nate. What are you going to do? Do you want to stay here or come back?"

"I'm going to have another look around, go back down to the road again."

"You are sure,?" I asked. "Let's at least try and get you a shirt, else you are going to get burned."

He nodded.

"I'll stay. Where do you think he is, Ani? Why hasn't he come up yet? Do you think he's survived?" His head was turning at the same time as talking to me as he miraculously hoped that the next turn of head would bring Fernando into his line of sight.

"Yes, why not, look how many people are still coming up to higher ground, there are families and loved ones being reunited all the time. Perhaps he got washed out to another part of the bay and it's taking him a bit longer, but he will come." I reassured him.

He nodded wanting to believe, willing it to be the truth, and he carried on calling, surveying the scene, looking for anyone that looked like him.

As I turned, I glimpsed the latest arrival of bodies. It was a sight I could barely bear to see. Tiny, lifeless innocent children looking like baby dolls were placed down on the floor, and my heart weighed heavily with grief.

I sobbed then.

"Why have we survived when all around us people have died?" I asked Nate.

"I question God, the Universe, myself, and everything. What cruel fate was this that families were ripped apart, children perished and me, a useless lump of a person has survived? Is there no justice in the world?"

Nate put his arm around me.

"Get out of here, Ani," he said. "It's too much to bear for anyone. I'm going to stay here for a while then head back to the road to see if I see him. I will find you in a bit."

I nodded, tears streaming down my face.

"Find me soon."

I headed back over to the clearing, which was a patch of grass on an otherwise sandy strip of land in a rough square shape where The Swedes were still giving first aid to everyone. I joined in aimlessly for a while, still racking my brain for how to get out of here.

I headed back to the jeep to listen to the latest news update at the top of the hour. New survivors had gathered around and now there were a dozen or more people congregating.

The latest news bulletin told me that there were some casualties being reported, up to 100s now from "a few." An international rescue effort was underway for affected countries. Reports of casualties on the train from Galle to Hikkaduwa as the wave had overturned the train and thousands were traveling at the time.

As I got down from the jeep, I announced to those around that were new or just wanted to hear again, "There was an earthquake off the coast of Indonesia, it's caused an Asian-wide tsunami. Thailand and India, as well as Sri Lanka and Indonesia, have been hit. Casualties are being reported in Indonesia, Sri Lanka, and Thailand. A rescue effort is underway, but choppers have been deployed to the south in Galle to help with a train overturned."

A murmur went around the gathered people, as various people started calling out.

"How do we get out of here?"

"The bridge has been destroyed, there was a fifth wave that destroyed it."

"We're stranded! How are we getting out of here?"

People panicked and hysterically started jostling and discussing how to get out.

"I don't know." I said despondently.

As I went around many of them would shout out at me, screaming "When is help coming?"

"When are we getting out of here?"

"I don't know," I replied, repeating all the information I knew, now like rote. "There's been an earthquake in

Indonesia, it's caused a tsunami and it's hit across Asia. We need to wait and be patient."

"It's not just us so it might take some time to get help here."

I'd inform them, so they at least had some of the same information as I.

Then suddenly I realised what needed to be done.

As a former BBC journalist, I knew that what gets reported bears little resemblance to what's really going on in the world. The stories that get reported are those that have your own nationals in them. A plane crash will get more news in the country if there are local people in that country that have been involved.

I needed to get the press on to the story and get some publicity for our plight.

I went over to Sri.

"I'm going to call the BBC. We need press coverage or publicity to get some help to get us out of here, otherwise we'll never get out."

Nate was in hearing distance and came over.

I started back towards the jeep to use the Norwegian's cell phone again.

Somehow, I managed to remember the number of the BBC switchboard in the recesses of my memory. As though my survival instinct knew this would be our only way out and found only the important bits of information I needed at this time. I was able to remember the number of the place I worked at five years earlier.

A small group of people had begun circling around me; many of them had been listening to my updates of what had happened.

I punched the numbers.

"BBC Switchboard," the operator's voice boomed.

"I need to speak to the news desk," I answered.

"Who can I connect you with?" The operator replied, not understanding the importance of my request or the frustration she was causing in me.

"I need the news desk; we've been caught in the tsunami in Sri Lanka, and we need help to get out of here."

"I'm sorry I can't connect you without a name."

My heart was racing.

"Look, it's Ani Naqvi. I used to work there, I'm a former BBC journalist and we must speak to a reporter. We've been in a tsunami. We're injured and there are some people who are going to die. You need to put me through to the news desk; it's a matter of life and death."

"I am sorry, Ani, I need a name to connect you." Again, the operator refused without a name.

"Tell them you're in the tsunami!" A bystander called out.

All around people were shouting out suggestions, hopeful of help through my call but not getting anywhere.

By now I was angry, after everything we'd been through, we were now about to be thwarted by a BBC switchboard operator? And then once again out of the depths of my memory I shouted a name.

"Mark Sandell!"

"Sorry?" the switchboard operator said.

"I'd like to speak to Mark Sandell."

Mark Sandell was my old editor when I'd worked with at the BBC on the Nicky Campbell show. Finally, the operator put me through.

The people surrounding me also didn't understand the red tape and were becoming incensed with the operator not putting me through to the news desk, but now I was getting somewhere.

I tried to relay the frustration to them all.

"I know this woman won't connect me without a name, but I've given her one now."

Nate was standing behind me now.

"Ani, tell them you're with Nate Berkus."

I glanced over at him.

He must have understood the perplexed look on my face and then he reiterated, "I'm on *The Oprah Winfrey Show*. I'm a TV presenter. Tell them you're with me, maybe they can get help?"

I stood back.

Oh, so he was a TV celebrity in the USA, and everyone knew Oprah. I turned back to the phone.

The dial tone at the other end of the phone kept ringing, why wasn't anyone answering? The noise in my ears was deafening as they rang out a high-pitched sound from where I feared my eardrum was busted.

Finally, someone answered.

"BBC News desk," a woman's voice answered.

"Mark Sandell," the words tumbled out of my mouth in a rush.

"Mark's on Christmas holidays," the voice offered. "Can I help at all? I'm Jo, one of the journalists working today."

"Hi, Jo, listen carefully. My name is Ani Naqvi. I used to work with Mark at BBC Radio 5 Live news. We've been caught in the tsunami on the east coast of Sri Lanka. There are around 400 people here, and we're on a remote part of the island. There are around 100 or so foreigners. We are stranded, and there's no way out. We need help. We're running out of clean water, and there's no food. We're trapped as the bridge in and out of the area has been destroyed."

The journalist couldn't believe her luck in what was turning out to be the main story of the day on an otherwise slow news day. Boxing Day, as the day after Christmas was called in the UK, had turned into the biggest news story ever.

The group around me was growing thicker as people craned their necks to hear the conversation, all shouting out their own thoughts and announcements. I was being jostled around.

"I need you to get me the number of the British High Commission or Foreign Office here in Sri Lanka to help get us out of here." I knew it was standard protocol that where possible the High Commission would do its best to look after the citizens of its nation and that help would be on hand. The British were very good for that. Their history of colonisation meant they had a significant presence around the world, Sri Lanka being one of them.

"Can I get an interview from you?" Jo asked.

"Yes. But I have a crowd of people around me waiting to use the phone to tell their loved ones they're OK and find out what's going on. Jo, people are dying all around us. If you get me the number of the High Commissioner or get him to call me on this number, I can give you an interview later, but right now this is a matter of life and death."

"Of course," she promised, "I'll see what I can do. I'll be back in touch soon."

"Here's the number to call us on," and I repeated the number to her.

As I hung up, I relayed the information to the crowd that had gathered around as word had travelled fast that I was in contact with the outside world via the BBC.

"Right all. I just spoke to the BBC. They are going to get in touch with the Foreign Office and the Consulate here and inform them of our plight. They will get someone from the Consulate to call us back on this phone shortly so I am hopeful we will get rescued soon."

"As soon as they call, I will let you know and give you the next update."

Nate approached me again.

"Hey, Ani, if I can connect with anyone at home, I can help get us out of here. Oprah knows people she can contact who will be able to help if you get the phone. I may be able to get help for all of us. I know I'm one person away from getting our coordinates to someone that can get us out of there."

I looked at Nate sideways, cautiously sizing this information up. Could he get us out of here? The US didn't have much of a presence in Sri Lanka not like the British did as an ex-colony, but if he really was famous would they send in special troops for him? I didn't recognise him personally, but that wasn't saying much.

I didn't want to discount anything that might help us, any potential leads that could get us out of there. So of course, it was a no-brainer, and I went to get the phone from the Norwegian again.

He was trying to conserve the battery so was limiting the use of his phone for people to call home, but this was vital.

"We need to use your phone again. Nate is famous in the States and knows Oprah Winfrey, who might be able to get us out of here, so he needs to use the phone to call for help."

"OK, but be careful of the battery and make it quick," the guy replied and handed the phone to me, and I passed it to Nate.

Nate began dialing. First, he dialed his mum and spoke carefully and firmly into the speaker.

"Mom, it's Nate here. You must listen very carefully. There has been a massive tsunami disaster in Sri Lanka. I want you to know that I am safe. Do not worry about me. I do not have a passport and I don't have anything right now, but there are several other people here from around the world. We have already notified the embassy."

A pause.

"Mom, I still can't find Fernando. He is missing. It happened hours ago, so I don't know where he would be. But I just wanted you to know that I am safe and fine. I will contact you when I have another opportunity; I borrowed this cell phone from someone. I love you."

Next, he called Oprah's people.

"Hey, this is Nate, I am alive and safe, our place was washed away by the tsunami here in Sri Lanka where I'm on vacation. I'm with a few dozen other tourists but we're stranded here as the bridge has been destroyed and there is no way to get out. I need you to get in touch with Oprah and see if we can get rescued here."

There was silence as the person at the other end spoke to Nate.

"Fernando is missing. We got separated and I haven't been able to find him here yet." His voice wavered.

"I'm fine, just a few scratches and bruises." I heard him reply and once I knew he'd relayed the most important information I stopped listening.

I knew how many resources someone like Oprah would have at her disposal and what she might do for one of her own, so at least there was a potential backup escape route if the High Commission didn't come through. The more people we told of our situation the quicker we would get help. Surely?

I stayed around the jeep waiting for the call back and still listening to the news and relaying it to new survivors as they made their way up.

TWELVE

We Start Documenting

I had to do something while waiting for the call back, so I decided I would make a list of the people that had survived, their relative countries of origin and the severity of their injuries. The information would be helpful to the High Commissioner when they eventually would call back.

My project management skills came into good use as I went around taking a register of the survivors.

"Hey what's your name? I'm taking a register for when we get rescued."

"My name is Simon Napper." He replied in a Southeast England accent.

"Are you British, Simon?"

"Yes?" He replied.

"How are you doing?"

"I'm OK. I can't really move at the moment though; I think I've broken my leg."

"Can I get you anything to make you more comfortable? Have you been seen by Anneli yet?"

"No, not yet."

"I'll call her for you, maybe she can put a splint on for you so it's a little more stabilised."

I went to as many people as I could, especially foreigners, as due to the language barrier I couldn't get much information from the local people. I was starting to feel the pain all over my body as I moved. The blood and mud on my face had caked up and I felt it pulling tightly on my skin, my calves and shins throbbing in pain, my cuts were oozing bloody pus, and my whole body now felt pummelled with pain.

Sometime later I had a long list, spanning a couple of pages of people from various nationalities.

I headed back towards Anneli.

"Anneli, how's it going? How is everyone?"

She gave me an update, which I logged.

"Most people have superficial injuries, but there's a woman with a serious head injury we have to get looked at, and there's an elderly man with a kidney infection that is going to die if we don't get medical help soon."

"I don't think there is anyone coming to rescue us just yet."

She nodded. Stefhan was behind her, supporting her every step of the way.

"There's also this small child that needs medical attention immediately; she's very badly injured."

It was bad enough that there were so many lost souls wandering around the place grief stricken and in shock. Now there were those that had survived that looked like they would die without medical attention.

I noticed many of the very seriously injured were Sri Lankan, so it was important to get their details registered too.

I began my next task to find someone local who spoke English to help me complete the register.

As I hobbled around, I called out to Sri Lankans, "English? Speak English?" I repeated.

Finally, one young Sri Lankan man who I also recognised called out, "Yes, I do," he volunteered.

"I need your help," I shouted. "We need to gather all the names of the living and their injuries. Can you help me?"

"Yes."

The two of us worked together.

Finally, the list was complete, well, as complete as it could be. We'd been to the people lying around in the clearing, and I'd diligently recorded as many details as I could.

There were around 400 of us, 300 locals and around 100 foreigners of various nationalities. Some Brits, Swedes, Dutch, Swiss, French and Israelis. There were people here from across the globe.

People were huddled together, looking for shade. Others were wandering around in a daze. Children were crying. There was total mayhem.

Hours had passed by now, and by the placement of the sun overhead, it looked like it was well into the late afternoon. I'd guess it was around 3:00 p.m. or 4:00 p.m. My mouth was parched from lack of water and talking. I was starting to wonder about basic supplies – but mostly water.

Finally, Jo from the BBC called back and asked to speak to me.

"Ani?"

"Yes, is that Jo?"

"Yes, I've spoken to the foreign office, and they have in turn assured me that they will get someone from the British High Commission in Sri Lanka to contact you soon. I have explained to them everything you told me, and you'll be expecting a call back imminently."

"Oh, thank you, Jo!" I cried, almost collapsing with relief.

"Is this a good time for that interview?" she replied.

I glanced around at the waiting crowd, and the low warning on the battery.

"Jo, I am so sorry. It's just that we don't have much battery left on this phone and we need to conserve it for the High Commissioner to contact us. But later when we have an exit plan for sure."

"Of course, I understand." she replied.

I turned to the crowd behind me.

"The British High Commission will be in touch soon." I shouted out to the bystanders listening in.

They looked as relieved as I felt. They may not be British but the fact that anybody cared meant a lot to us.

Finally, the phone rang.

The Norwegian waved me over.

"Ani, it's for you!"

Relieved, I took the phone.

"Hi. Is that Ani?"

"Yes."

"This is Colin Stevens, I'm from the High Commission, I'm the Deputy High Commissioner. How are you? I understand you've been in the tsunami and spoken with the BBC and there are a few of you stranded over in Arugam Bay?"

"Yes, there are around 400 of us here and around hundred or so foreigners from around the globe," I was rushing the information out.

"Most of us are Europeans. There is also a famous American, Nate Berkus, who appears on *The Oprah Winfrey Show,* and we're stranded here with no way in or out," my words tumbled out in a rush.

"There are many severely injured people who need medical attention and need to be airlifted out."

"Don't worry, Ani, we are on it. We are working on a rescue plan, and we will get you out. Unfortunately, it will not happen tonight. It's too late to get the choppers deployed to you now as it will become dark soon." My heart plummeted and I groaned internally.

"There was a widespread disaster, and the Sri Lankan government sent the helicopters to the south and other areas where there were a large number of casualties. It's looking like an international crisis, so resources are limited but I promise you we'll get you all out."

Big pools of water began to pierce my eyes as his reassuringly British upper-class accent, calm demeanour, and warm voice allowed my guard to slip as hope finally began to trickle into me.

"When can you get the choppers here?"

"We won't be able to send them till the morning now as by the time they get there it will be dark, and it's dangerous for them to fly in the dark. Will you be able to manage till morning?"

My heart sunk once more. Morning, I thought, stranded here till morning. NO I silently screamed. Around me people had gathered, and everyone was listening with bated breath, silently knowing this was their chance of rescue as they knew this was our best and only hope of making it out.

"Not really. We don't have any drinking water, food, or clothes. We don't have a phone other than this, and the battery is low. We don't have anything; how can we stay here?"

"I can arrange for some water and basic supplies to be sent by the army and maybe some lunch packets if that helps."

"How can they get here if the bridge has gone?"

"There are troops in the area already." Colin reassured me.

"OK, hold on, let me tell the others."

I turned to the growing crowd. They were silent and waiting for the information.

"They can't send choppers till the morning, but they can send an army vehicle with some basic supplies."

A groan went around.

"Get them to bring cigarettes," someone called out. There was laughter.

"Colin, please get the army to bring us some cigarettes, too."

He chuckled.

"Will do, is there anything else you need that I can get them to bring for you?"

"We don't have a phone, this one I am using is running out of battery. How will I communicate with you?"

"I'll send over a phone to you, as well. It will be a satellite phone so you can get in touch with me, and I'll work on sending the choppers over to you as soon as dawn breaks. Stay put and well done. You're doing a great job. We'll be there soon. You've all been very brave and are doing amazingly well. We will come for you as soon as it is safe to do so."

"OK," I replied numbly.

"I'll give you a call back shortly, let me make some calls and I'll be in touch when I have more information"

As I hung up the phone, I announced it to everyone, "That was the British Deputy High Commissioner. He's aware of the situation and will send some choppers out in the morning to airlift the wounded to Ampara, the nearest army medical centre."

"Morning? What are we to do until then? We have no food or supplies," a man called out angrily.

"We have to stay put and wait."

"What if they don't come?" Another person called out, scared.

"They will, he promised me. It's the British High Commission. I'm sure they will. We just have to sit tight, make camp for the night, and by dawn break we'll be rescued."

I was exhausted, drained, and it took all my might to not let my own voice crack under the pressure. I kept my voice as calm as I could, aware of the hysteria that could take over the whole group if I let my own panic show. I was starting to see that the crowd viewed me as the person in control, phoning, making lists, in the know, coming up with ideas to get us out of here, if I crumbled, they too could follow suit. I tried to be as strong and dependable as I could even if I felt myself crumble inside.

I was used to portraying a strong veneer and right in that moment it was exactly what was called for and so I plastered confidence on my face and kept the veneer up.

I looked around. Sri was sitting at the side of the clearing with Duncan's three children who hadn't stopped sobbing since they'd made it to higher ground. Annelli and Stefhan were moving back to their spot at the makeshift clinic. Nate was standing next to Sri.

"Sri, what happened to the other people staying at Galaxy? Have you any word yet, what about the doctors next to me, they could help us?"

"They didn't make it." Sri said with her head down. "Neither did most of the family of nine in number 1 hut."

A chill went down my spine, and despite the hot day my skin had goosebumps and my hairs stuck up from the news. The little babies with big brown eyes and kohl under their eyes were probably no more. My heart broke at the tragedy of three whole generations being killed at once.

There was a long heavy silence as a wave of sadness and hopelessness washed over us once more.

Nate was still looking around, eyes peeled for Fernando, heavy with glistening tears ready to fall. Suddenly he stood up straight.

"Oh, thank God, there are the Squires."

He rushed off to a middle-aged white male and a diminutive blond woman who looked very badly injured.

As I sat quietly watching, more and more people came up to me to ask what was going on. I repeated the same thing over and over, my voice becoming hoarse from retelling the same thing.

Eventually I got up. I went over to the clearing where most of the people were gathered to tell them all.

"Everyone listen up," I shouted. "Here is the latest news. I've been in touch with the BBC who contacted the British High Commission on our behalf. I have also personally spoken to the Deputy High Commissioner, who has assured me they will get us out of here at first light tomorrow."

I paused.

A cacophony of voices chimed in as people started throwing out questions and objections.

"Morning? We're stranded here till morning. Why aren't they coming now?"

"It's too late for them to send the choppers now as it's getting dark, and they can't fly at night. Added to that they sent most of them to the south where there were mass casualties. So, it will take them time to get here and it's too dangerous for them now." I replied.

"But we have no water, no food, no shelter?"

"Colin, the High Commissioner, will send some water and other supplies with an army jeep soon before it gets too dark. But we're going to have to camp out here for the night." I pointed in the direction of the clearing where the sheets and blankets were set up.

Angry, disturbed voices discussed this latest turn of events but what else could we do? We were on such a remote part of the island, so far from civilization this was the best that Colin could do.

Sri Lanka is so close to the equator that sunrise and sunset didn't vary much throughout the year. They were at approximately 6:00 a.m. – 6:00 p.m. and as the light dimmed, I finally had a sense of time. Dusk was a quick affair here; within an hour it would be pitch black with the light of the stars and moon to show the way. Luckily temperatures didn't drop that much at night, and it was usually a low of 24 with a high of 33 all year round so at least we wouldn't freeze.

I urged people to start to prepare for the long night out as they took up places to lie on the uneven ground, huddling around each other for warmth as dusk began.

Some people began to sort out wood for fires, while others got clothes and sheets together, as a makeshift camp started to come together.

Nate headed to the vacant minister's house who had been airlifted with the first chopper which had brought such hope with it only to be dashed when it headed off without us. He went with some other people to grab sheets and blankets and on arrival placed them on the floor and gave them to those severely injured or in shock.

Once the blankets were distributed, we made camp on the hard, bumpy piece of land. I had nothing to sit on but a thin sheet. Even though it was warm and balmy, I felt myself shaking for the first time. I settled down next to Nate and we discussed his search for Fernando.

"He will come," I told him with my arm around him. "It has only been about 10 hours since the wave hit Nate. He may have been picked up by a rescue team already and flown off for all we know."

He nodded. I was glad for the dimming light, knowing it was hiding my doubt.

THIRTEEN

Threats of Another Wave

"Sandra?"

"Sam?"

"Sarah?"

"Mark?"

Weak, panicked, heartbroken voices continued their desperate search as parents frantically searched for missing children, wives for their lost husbands, and men for their families.

"Where is he, Ani?" Nate asked for the thousandth time.

"Maybe he got knocked unconscious and is lying somewhere and waiting to be found, or he could have been washed into the jungle and is trying to make his way out." I tried to placate him.

As we sat, the sky turned into its characteristic pink, peach, and lilac hues like a painting from Monet. And just like that dusk was upon us; it wouldn't be long before the sky would turn inky blue with the orange moon hanging over the shoreline like a low-lying piece of fruit ready to be picked. The full moon in the tropics and in Arugam Bay was a blood orange colour. When it would first rise, it would glisten against the sea reflecting its luminosity in a dreamy way, usually the lap of the ocean and the moon making a beautiful backdrop.

As the dark came, the cries got quieter. All day there had been a frantic search for the living, and the village had entertained an endless stream of people hobbling, crying, or wailing.

The noise was dimming now. Everything slowed down, and the bodies stopped arriving. It was now impossible for those Sri Lankan heroes to keep going to pick up the bodies in the dark. They, too, stopped their work and the night settled around us all.

Some fishermen had got a fire going and were barbecuing some lobsters over by the clearing.

Sri was sitting next to me, her eyes vacant.

"There is some crazy irony of being stranded in a scene of devastation while there is lobster being grilled," I said.

Lobster, normally the food for the rich, was being simply served out in tasty morsels by these Sri Lankan fisher folks.

No one believed anything anymore, the very nature of the fabric of our worlds turned inside out, upside down, unstitched and unravelling.

I headed back towards Nate and Sri as we leaned on each other for comfort. I was spent and needed a break. There we sat in our own reveries, Nate with thoughts of Fernando,

Sri surveying the scene quietly looking for the highest point in case she needed to make another run for it. There was nowhere for us to rest our back on, and sitting on the ground was painful and uncomfortable.

I looked down at my legs. They were throbbing and there was a red ooze of blood mixed with white, putrefying puss. I knew my face was swollen; one eye was barely open from the bruising and half of the skin had been scraped away. But I could barely feel the wounds. My entire body was still in survival mode.

Claudia, Duncan's other daughter, was with her now, crying helplessly, frantically repeating over and over and over again that we were all going to die. They had a terrible tale of survival involving snake bites, buildings they were holding onto disintegrating, and a long path back to safety that we would find out over the next few days.

Suddenly, a noise broke through the quiet village. It was a car motor. I stood up and an army jeep suddenly appeared around a corner.

I headed over as the jeep came round.

"Which one of you is Ani?" they called.

"Me," I replied as I walked over to them.

"These are for you" – he handed over bottles of water, some lunch packets, and packs of cigarettes.

"We're going to need you to all come with us, though," the army guy said.

"Where to?" I asked warily.

"We've heard reports of another tsunami coming," he said within earshot of everyone else.

Suddenly, there was another wave of panic and tension as people shrieked and screamed.

"We've been instructed to take you to a place that is even higher than here."

"Where is it?"

"Along the seafront on top of a cliff in Panama," they replied.

"NO!" a sea of voices around me shouted, the thought and fear of having to go near the shoreline terrifying them all.

I looked around at them and at the same time the Israeli woman and French man were on either side of my flank grabbing my right and left arm, digging their fingers in so much that it bruised my already tender, beaten, and bruised flesh. Both hysterically shouting at me that they didn't want to go. Their grip was painful as in their fear they forgot their own strength.

Meanwhile, one of Duncan's daughters was standing on my right foot and clamped onto my right leg for dear life. Sobbing, she looked up at me with her huge blue eyes, pools of tears dropping down her face. Her face was smudged with black, mud, and tears on her normally rosy face. "No, Ani, please. I don't want to go!" The little girl pleaded with me.

The Israeli lady was wiry and bird-like, slim in her late 40s, and she was talking rapidly, her words like bullets from an AK47. On the other arm was an older French man with dark hair, greying temples, and a salt and pepper beard. He was holding my arm too tightly, gripping me, digging his fingers into me as though I was life itself. Such was their panic and expectation from me that I felt the pressure and burden firmly on my shoulders.

Both older, they pleaded with me as though I was somehow in charge or had the power to make this decision on their behalf, and I realised that having taken on the role of news announcer and getting in touch with the BBC and foreign office they had cast me in the role of someone who knew how and what to get done. My actions had given them hope, and I realised I almost had a duty and responsibility to fulfill to get them out of there as safely as possible.

They were looking to me to tell them what to do, and I couldn't at that moment tell them to go with the army not until I had verified the information thoroughly.

"Who is telling you this?" I asked the army officer.

"The Sri Lankan government," they replied. I thought for a moment, my instincts sending me messages. Hmm, I wasn't sure I fully trusted what these guys were saying. My journalistic instinct kicked in, and I realised what I needed to do. I needed to verify the source of this information. I knew from having worked in news when reporting on previous disasters that sometimes there was misinformation in the aftermath of a disaster that wasn't true.

I could check by contacting the BBC again as I knew they would have had a slew of seismologists on through the day. The BBC would have triple fact checked their stories and know if there really was a risk or not. I trusted the BBC as much as I could trust anything at that moment.

Besides, everyone was refusing to move. Others had gathered around me, crying and hysterical, pleading with me to not make them move as they didn't want to leave to go to higher ground or anywhere near the seashore where the horror of the tsunami and what it had ripped them of clearly showed in their fearful eyes and the trembling of their hands.

I went to get the phone and called out to everybody around.

"OK, everyone, let me call the BBC again. They will be able to verify whether these reports of another tsunami are true or not. If they say not then maybe we don't have to leave here."

"Yes, yes, we don't want to leave," a chorus of chattering as people's attention focused on what I said, and they eagerly and nervously waited in anticipation.

The young daughter Sasha, of Duncan, the tabloid journalist, was still sobbing and clutching on to my leg for dear life. She was around 5 years old, with dirty blonde hair, a rosy-cheeked face smeared with dirt, and hair matted and awry. She had lost her family during the wave and had fallen into the water alone but managed to grab hold of the back of a fridge to keep her afloat. The fridge had become wedged between two trees and had stopped her, but it was a while before the family found her.

"Please don't make us go! We don't want to leave here; get us out of here, Ani!" She pleaded with me again.

She was not the only one grabbing at me.

The grown-ups were grabbing me, too, frantic with worry and despair, repeating the same pleas of the little girl at the same time.

Sasha clung to me like a limpet as I attempted to move with her holding on tightly to my leg. I put my hand on her head and tried to comfort and reassure her that everything would be OK. I was not a mother, so this was a new challenge to me. She was in pain. A plank of wood had slammed into her, and she had been forced to pull a nail out of her foot whilst the water tried to drag her back into the torrent.

The poor mite had suffered so much already mother or not my maternal instincts wanted to do whatever I could to alleviate any further suffering for her. My heart went out to her as a little girl who had survived so much already for her tender years. Surely any parent's worst nightmare.

I decided my only way forward was to get the information straight. This time I had a phone! The army had delivered not only the cigarettes but a satellite phone for me.

I dialed Jo the journalist's number again.

"Jo, we have the army here and they're telling us there will be another tsunami and want to move us to higher ground along the shore. Can you confirm this is true?"

"Give me a second." There was a long pause then. "No, Ani, we've had a number of eyewitness reports of mass hysteria in Sri Lanka that there is another wave, but there is no evidence to suggest that is the case from a scientific point of view. None of our seismologists are predicting this is the case."

I breathed out in relief.

"So, we can stay where we are and not move?" I asked.

There was a collective sigh of relief around me as people craned to hear my side of the conversation.

"Well, at the BBC they are not getting these reports, so it does just seem like there is mass hysteria in the country. Probably misinformation."

"Thanks, Jo."

"Can I get that interview now?" she asked again.

"Sure, call me back shortly. Let me just let everyone know this news."

"OK – how long?"

"Give me an hour."

"OK, Ani. I'll call back then."

As I hung up, people surrounded me in a circle. I called out to the crowd.

"Listen up, everyone. I've just spoken to the BBC. They are saying there are NO reports of another tsunami and it's just eyewitness reports of mass hysteria that are spreading this rumour. But their seismologists are denying this is the case, so we can stay here if we want."

There were hushed voices.

"How do we know they're true, though?" A man angrily called out.

"I know the BBC checks their facts thoroughly, so I am confident if they say there isn't going to be another tsunami then there won't be; but if you don't believe that, then let me check with Colin, the British High Commissioner, and see what he says. Then we can decide. You are, of course, welcome to go with the army, though, if you wish to. The decision is yours, and that's the same for all of you."

I turned back to the phone and dialed Colin's number.

"Colin?"

"Hi, Ani."

"We're all in a bit of a panic here. The army has arrived and told us to leave to go to Panama, a nearby town, as there is another wave coming. But to get there we must travel along the shore, and everyone's freaking out here. No one wants to go anywhere near the sea again, as you can imagine. Can you confirm if this information is true? I just called the BBC, but they're saying it's not. These army guys are saying another wave is going to come at 1:00 a.m. and it's going to be even bigger than the ones we've already had."

My words came out in a huge rush as panic coursed through my veins. I also knew the entire crowd was listening, so I wanted to be accurate and careful. Still stuck to my leg was the little girl, and I didn't want to scare her.

Colin cleared his throat.

"No, we don't think these reports are true, Ani. If you guys want to stay where you are, that should be fine. We have heard the Sri Lankan government issuing this warning, but the British Foreign Office is not corroborating their version of events, and our own sources agree with the BBC. We do think the tsunami is over. We can't guarantee it, as this is a new situation we've never faced before but as far as we know, it's false."

I breathed out.

"Are you sure, Colin? There are a lot of lives at stake here."

"With the information we have to hand, as sure as we can be."

"OK, thanks, I'll let them know."

A huge sigh of relief emanated from me as I turned to the crowd. The thought of being moved somewhere at this time of the day after everything we'd been through back towards the sea would be very challenging. I didn't know if I had it in me; I was barely holding it together as it was.

"Hey, everyone, the BBC and the British High Commission have both denied this report of another tsunami coming at 1:00 a.m. It seems like panic and misinformation, and they say the event is over. So, if you want to stay here, you can. If you are worried, then go with the army to higher ground."

There was murmuring around as everyone began to talk. But most of them moved back to the fire.

Meanwhile, my eyes began to scour the scene, automatically searching for even higher ground just in case the BBC were wrong. I spied a tall coconut tree and wondered if I could climb to the top as I looked at its branches and questioned whether I had the strength to do so.

I glanced around at the tops of the buildings noting which was the tallest and if it would be enough to save me from another potential deadly wave.

This was what many of us would do in those hours as we sought out survival once more.

Everyone else seemed to feel the same as me, too drained, exhausted, and horrified at going anywhere near the sea again.

I had kept the phone, but people were clamouring around to use it so they could call home to verify this information from their own countries, but they struggled to remember numbers and called family to get updates instead.

Our nerves were so on edge by now that there was no modicum of politeness. Survival was the name of the game and while some people exhibited some noble and selfless behaviours, others were the opposite, and the worst examples of that were yet to come.

I left them to it and hobbled off back to Nate and Sri and tried to take solace in them, leaving the others behind.

After I got off the phone to Colin, I began to sit down on the hard, uneven brush-like floor. No sooner had I done so that the phone rang again. This time it was Jo, the journalist from the BBC, calling for her interview I'd promised.

"Is that Ani?"

"Yes," I replied wearily.

"Is this a good time to do the interview?" she asked. I replied yes and spent the next few minutes occupied with that.

FOURTEEN

The Long Night Out on The Hill - A Review of the Survivors

We settled in for the night, and I did a walkabout and took stock.

There were a few severely injured people in the clinic I knew of. There was an older Sri Lankan man with kidney disease who was almost dead. There was a small child with a horrific head wound, blood seeping out from her makeshift bandage.

Then I walked past a woman with a broken leg. Nate had joined me in the walkabout.

"She was sucked down a well," he told me. "Her fiancé was missing for most of the day, but just a few hours ago he walked up here."

I had heard that earlier.

They'd embraced in relief when they once again found each other, and a huge cheer had emanated from the crowd. They had taken much solace from a family being reunited and it lifted our despair and spirits, giving us some much needed hope.

We were all holding on for a happy story of reuniting, so when it came it was a genuine feeling of buoyancy.

We walked past Simon Napper. I had found out that Simon was actually a British skateboarder who'd won a ton of awards in his youth and was a mini celebrity. He was now lying with a broken leg and a makeshift splint made from a piece of wood Stefhan had found. Simon had been living at Siam View, another hotel in the middle of the bay, when the tsunami had hit.

He relayed tales of being lifted up while he was sleeping with his mattress under him and being washed out with the wave like we had. Unfortunately, the mattress disappeared soon after, and he had to fight to stay afloat in the water's power.

Nate and I walked over to a family he had connected with. Nate had taken up camp with the Squire family of five. They had all been holidaying at the same hotel and had known him and Fernando. During that long night they told us about their day.

The Squire family — composed of the father Phillip, the mother Louise, and kids Emma, Laura and Will — had been to Sri Lanka many times, and this was their second trip to Arugam Bay. They were in the hotel restaurant when the tsunami hit. They were separated within seconds.

Initially, they all thought they were the lone survivors. But slowly, as the first wave receded, the kids and Phil found each other. Then it was only mum Louise who was still missing. It had taken hours to find her. She had climbed up a tree and waited out the wave, but she had been bitten by a snake up in the trees. Despite the pain and fear, she held on while the water was still high. I couldn't imagine the horror of being not only in a tsunami but to then find yourself wrestling with a snake for survival, too, and getting bitten! I mean, it didn't get much worse than that frankly. I felt I had gotten off lightly in comparison. But luckily, this story had one of the few happy endings as the entire family was reunited over the next few hours.

Phil had taken a paternal watch over Nate and had a terrible foot injury and could barely walk.

Nate had first spotted Louise Squire but prevented himself from asking about Fernando as he said her eyes looked even more haunted than he had imagined his own were. They had all met Fernando and knew what he looked like, so he knew they'd recognise him if he were found.

We all gathered for the night, and my small band of survivors had grown bigger.

It was clear this news from the army had rattled everyone to his or her core. Not only had we survived not one but seven huge tsunamis, we now were faced with our next challenge. If I didn't know better, I would have thought this was some weird and sadistic game show.

It was still early and throughout the evening Colin called regularly to update me on the latest and keep us reassured. I held on to those calls and his voice as a lifeline, desperate to get out of there but unable to, trapped in our own world of hell. We must have spoken around a dozen times or so that evening and all through the night.

I was too wired to sleep. Most of us were. The adrenaline in our systems was coursing through keeping us alive, keeping the pain of our injuries at bay as they throbbed in the background. The surroundings were bleak and dismal, and we sat all night waiting impatiently for dawn to come.

Others, like Sri, on the other hand, went and sat quietly, contemplating their escape routes.

"Ani, I feel so terrible," she whispered. "What about the families in my hotel? What about all the children and babies in hut number 1?"

I took her hand, aghast at the memory. The image of the little babies playing in the sand with their kohl eyeliner eyes. I remembered them looking so content as they sat there in the sand playing with their mums. My heart broke once more into another thousand pieces.

"Oh, God, did all nine die?"

She shook her head.

"Not all. The older family members who survived are here."

I stared at her.

We were all just trying to manage our shock and terror in our own ways. Sri was quiet, racked with guilt and a sense of responsibility for her guests, while I busied myself with all these small but useful activities – making lists, checking on bodies, and liaising with the outside world. This was my coping mechanism, staying busy, taking charge, making lists. It's what kept me from falling back into the abyss I had found myself in at the very beginning when Sri had left me with the kind man on my own. That sense of helplessness and despair that had overtaken me was even scarier, which is why staying busy and active helped keep me together.

I looked around at the faces in the camp. Some were struggling and were also angry, lashing out at others, whilst others comforted children and adults and kept hope alive.

One woman stood out. She sat down in the clearing and made little straw dolls with twigs and leaves. The children all gathered around her like the Pied Piper and sat down with her while she showed them how to make these pretty little dolls. She was so beautifully calm and emanated a wise, serenity that was exactly what these children needed, something to occupy their minds and hands and dull the trauma and abate the tears for a few minutes. Many of them were alone, in shock, and the only survivors of a family.

She was like an angel of children sitting there. I realised that there were many angels all around who stood up and were there to help others. The tsunami brought out the best and the worst in humanity. Fear overtaking the sensibilities of man in this stripped-down horror version of life.

FIFTEEN

Dreams and Horrors

I tried to sleep, but not a soul slept on the hill that night. This was not new to me. I had battled to sleep for decades. I never slept well – a hangover from my childhood where I lived on eggshells due to a difficult and temperamental father. An accumulation of living like this for 16 years had taken its mental toll on me.

Between whispered conversations, my mind raced back over my 30 years on this planet so far.

Mum and Dad were both born in India, two hours north of Delhi, and that's where our heritage originated. After the Second World War, in 1947, India descended into chaos as it ceased to exist as a British colony. World War II had severely damaged the British Empire in terms of economy, and they had to relinquish many of their colonies.

In its place were created two separate sovereign states – India and Pakistan.

After thousands of years of living peacefully with each other Hindus and Muslims were at each other's throats.

Both my parents were children at the time, and the area wasn't safe for them being of Muslim descent. So, their families migrated across to the newly formed Pakistan, the country carved out for Muslims to escape while millions lost their lives in the battles over that tumultuous period.

Coming from a typical Asian family, my father wanted me to follow in his footsteps and become a barrister. But the vagaries of the law, defending potentially guilty criminals or putting away potentially innocent ones and ruining their lives, didn't sit well with my sense of justice. Neither did I want to be a part of. My father and I had a tumultuous relationship at best, and I had no desire to satisfy his wishes, rather the opposite. I showed my defiance and will by being the opposite of the subservient daughter.

I was born in London, in Clapham, and spent the first three years of my life growing up in Balham before moving to Tooting Broadway until I was 13. After that, my parents moved to Cheam, in Surrey.

Failing to go into law, my parents wanted me to be a doctor, engineer, or even accountant. Not dissimilar to many Asian families. I had one sister who was much younger than I.

However, heavily influenced by Michael Buerk's Ethiopia famine story that sparked Live Aid in 1988 and Kate Adie's Tiananmen Square massacre story in 1989, I chose journalism instead as a young teenager.

Kate Adie was my hero – a fearless warrior, a foreign correspondent who would end up in the worst and most dangerous spots around the world, reporting from the front line. After the disappointment of my mother and my perceived weakness of her for not leaving an abusive husband, Kate was the perfect antithesis.

I thought they were changing the world –but realised years later the world was the same. There was still famine in Africa, for example. I'd nobly and naively thought that being a journalist and bringing the "truth" to people's homes would have the power to change things – unfortunately this wasn't the case.

My dad left the UK when I was 16, finally allowing me to be free. Mum followed him after my first year at university. She'd been made redundant from her job at Morgan Stanley, and my sister Anita, who was 10 years my junior, hadn't managed to get into her first-choice school. So, Mum decided it was best to follow my dad back to Pakistan. I was settled at university; I'd made friends and I was on the degree course I wanted. I'd admittedly not come back much in the holidays, having too much fun in Bristol, which had an amazing music scene back in the early '90s.

Mum and I had rowed about her decision. I thought she was crazy to follow him back to Pakistan and to drag my poor sister along with her and had told her as much. "How could you do this to Anita," I'd screamed at her. "Wasn't it enough that I had to put up with his behaviour, but now you want to inflict that on her, too?"

Growing up as an Asian, racism was the norm, the calls of "Paki" from classmates singling me out and highlighting my difference, even though I never really saw myself like that.

I realised the mainstream news, even the BBC that had been my source of respect as a bastion of fair, impartial news back then, was not at all what I had expected. It had a skewed right-wing agenda – as did most, if not all, of the press. The news wires would give a clear indication of what was really going on in the world, but what got reported on was a tiny sliver of that.

Working as a journalist had been a wildly exciting, adrenaline-fueled time, reacting to breaking news, getting reporters out on the scene, interrupting a programme in the middle to cut to a plane crash or other big breaking story, yet inside I felt a disconnect.

As a journalist your reaction to a plane crash isn't "oh the poor victims," it's about how big the story is. Should we bump it to the top of the running order? Who should we get on the scene? When should we interrupt the program?

Everything is a story. People become stories, natural disasters, everything ready to be exploited and provided to the consumer as entertainment wrapped up in news.

You need to develop a thick skin and remove yourself from the tragedy otherwise it will eat you up inside. Many journalists develop a thick skin, but I never managed to truly master this, even though I thought I had.

Working in news and realising the right-wing bias, I also noticed the bias against ethnic minorities and the differences in reporting based on ethnicity, race, or sex.

I don't know why I was so shocked by this, but I was. It enraged my sense of injustice and unfairness.

This was back at the end of 1999, and I was outraged then. But what could I do?

I finally left the BBC under a cloud of disillusionment. I wanted to spend New Year's to welcome the new millennium in Sydney and work on the Sydney Olympics Project, and both these intentions came true. I climbed on the top of a bus to watch the fireworks over Sydney Harbour and the bridge.

This led me into another line of work, project work. I decided that rather than just report on the news I would get into project work and try to change things and deliver real projects with impact.

So that was where I was in my life. Working on projects in the public sector.

And now, as I sat under the open stars on that hill, I knew nothing would ever be the same again.

SIXTEEN

Day 2: A Waiting Game

As dawn started to break, I began calling Colin again. It was around 5:00 in the morning by now, and my eyes scanned the skies as the inky black sky started to give way to a deep blue at first then a lighter blue. Yet I couldn't hear any choppers.

"Where are the choppers, Colin?"

"You should hear them any second. Ani, can you remind me of how many of you are there? I didn't make a note last time in the chaos."

"There are around 400 local people, around 15 are seriously injured, 3 critically. Then there are around 100 foreign tourists, all from different countries, a few Brits, Swedes, Americans, and other nationalities. Some of them are severely injured. A few were taken on the chopper yesterday, but most are here."

"Good, well done. That's very good we have that information; it will help us plan how to get you out and provide facilities for you all when you're airlifted."

"Do you want to know the names and nationalities of the foreigners?" I asked. I've taken a makeshift register if that helps."

"Yes, please. We can get in touch with their relevant embassies and coordinate with them."

I started down the list.

- Nate Berkus, USA
- Sri Gunasena UK
- Anneli Onneby, Sweden
- Stefhan Markstrom, Sweden
- Simon Napper, UK
- Duncan and Penney Ridgley, UK, and kids Angus, Claudia, and Sasha
- Philip Squire, UK
- Louise Squire, UK, plus Emma, Laura and Will Squire

On and on I went, reeling off a list of names to Colin as he noted them down.

These types of activities kept what little sanity I had left intact on that long night. Keeping myself useful was my lifeline, otherwise I would go into a void and never come back again. So mentally shaken I was, holding on to these small semblances of normality were what held me together.

Anneli glanced down at my list of the injured, who would take first place on the choppers.

"We need to get the people who are critical out first, otherwise they might not make it," we said to each other.

"So let's put them in order of injury severity." I started organising the names so that once the choppers were here the people with the most severe injuries would get airlifted first. There had already been so much death we didn't want more people dying on us.

I compiled the list by getting the information from Anneli, as she had seen most of the injured people. We busied ourselves with these tasks, which took another hour or two – a much needed and welcome distraction from confronting the horrors of the past 24 hours.

We lined up the people to go on the first choppers as per the list and reassured the people that help was coming soon.

I called Colin again.

"Where are they, Colin?"

His calm voice soothed my jangled nerves.

Fear that they weren't actually coming was seeping through me.

"Close, Ani. In fact, you should hear them coming right now." Sure enough, as soon as he said that, with my eyes peeled to the sky, I started to hear the distant whirr of the helicopters in the distance. I almost sobbed with relief.

Trauma, shock, there is no way to know how you will react until you face it. It doesn't matter what you think you'll do; what you actually do is very different.

When in my depression I'd think I was useless and didn't deserve to live, I'd remind myself of my instincts in a disaster. They say that how you act in a disaster is your true nature coming out. If that were true, then I couldn't be as bad as I thought I was, could I?

SEVENTEEN

Rescued

Finally the noise of the choppers got louder. Shouts went up from our band of bedraggled survivors.

Everyone started to stand up, and a ripple of muted cheers went around as people realised their ordeal was nearly over. Anneli and I busied ourselves sorting out the waiting queue of injured.

Suddenly, there was a rush of movement as the first chopper landed rapidly and people started to run towards it. These people were not the injured who could barely move.

I watched in horror as I realised that these people would delay those who were injured from getting on.

I was embarrassed watching the scene. The fact that people were running meant that physically they were OK when so many others weren't. I noted that it was mostly tourists, and the Sri Lankans didn't behave like that. In fact, the Sri Lankans had been kind and empathetic to us all through the night, feeding us, taking care of us, clothing us. They stood back watching the scene unfold.

It felt like all our efforts were being thwarted. Trying to take charge and control who got onto the choppers in the order of injury was thrown out the window as people raced to survival.

My face was puce with disbelief as I ran to the chopper with a young army soldier standing outside with a machine gun. I squared up to him shouting over the din of the blades.

"Why are you letting these people on? You need to take these injured people first as they will die otherwise."

He looked at me blankly. He couldn't have been more than 19 years old. He was tall, which was unusual. He towered above me, his Kalashnikov in his hand, while I shouted over the din of the choppers. But he was young and inexperienced. No one had ever had to deal with a disaster of this magnitude, and my words fell on deaf ears. It dawned on me that the Sri Lanka army would want to get the tourists out to avoid international condemnation.

Before I knew it, the first helicopter was off and away as I helplessly watched on, boiling over. I ran to the next chopper and tried to convey the same message. In the meantime, Anneli and some Sri Lankans were bringing over the injured people to the chopper.

Suddenly, there was a fracas behind. The Frenchman who had been gripping my arm earlier the night before was squaring up to Anneli and shouting at her.

"Who are you to tell me I can or can't go on the helicopter?" he was yelling.

He was tall, around 6 ft and menacing in his fear and anger. Anneli was a petite woman, and there he was looking like he was about to punch her.

"Hey!"

I shouted and put myself in between them. "Don't shout at her. She has been the only one who has been looking after everyone and giving first aid, and you have the nerve to shout at her." I tried to make myself big as my protection for Anneli made me stronger.

I couldn't believe it. Where was the gratitude or the acknowledgment of the selfless work Anneli had done all day? Without her, none of us would have had any medical treatment. In hindsight, I realised that fear makes us all act out of terror and that these responses were normal given the circumstances.

"I want to get on the chopper. I have my family here and my children. We have to get out."

"We all want to get out; the choppers will come all day long until everyone has gone. Just let these sick people go and I promise you your family can go on the next chopper that comes."

He ignored me and Anneli, and running, he grabbed his family, and they ran for the next chopper.

The army was overwhelmed with dealing with any kind of crowd control or organisation for this scenario. The magnitude of the disaster was the biggest the world would ever see. There were no tsunami plans in place or a playbook of what one should do in such circumstances, and I realised everyone was doing the best they could in extraordinary times.

Most of the tourist families that were intact had run to get on the choppers. The only ones who held back were those still waiting for their loved ones. Finally, we were able to get the sick and injured on board. The little girl with the head wound boarded, and I so wished and hoped she'd make it through. It would be a tense few days before we would find out her fate.

We tried to keep some semblance of order as we indicated to the people on our lists who was next based on the severity of their condition, and Sri Lankan men carried the worst injured on their makeshift stretchers to the choppers carefully one by one.

I made my way over to each person with my list indicating to them they were next to get airlifted.

I was shouting instructions over the din of the rotor blades. The whole scene was chaotic with running tourists and beds being carried by Sri Lankan men running to get the injured onboard.

"Who's next?" Anneli shouted at me as I had the list.

"It's Simon." As I went up to him to start to get him on the chopper, we spoke.

"OK, Simon, you're on next."

"No, it's OK. I'll stay,

"What do you mean?"

"I'll wait for the next one or one later."

"But you've got a broken leg." I looked at him surprised.

"It's OK, I'll manage. It's just a leg. There are far worse injuries than mine," he said. Tears pricked my eyes, and in that one instant he restored my wavering faith in humanity.

I set off to gather the next on the list.

The morning continued until we'd managed to get many of the 100s of people on the choppers. It was endless, and chopper after chopper landed.

By now, I was exhausted. It was immensely stressful work, and I was beginning to unravel. Tired, hungry, thirsty, hot, and traumatised, I'd expended so much energy trying to control the situation, which I couldn't as everything was beyond my control. Ever since the tsunami had struck, it was a potent lesson that we control none of our external surroundings, only our reactions to them.

I ran back to where Sri was to check up on her, "Sri, you can get on the next chopper."

"No, I'm OK," she replied.

"But you're pregnant, you should go, just in case there's something wrong with the baby. You should get yourself checked out."

"No. I'm OK, I'll stay here with you."

A deep sense of relief came to me that she would stay with me and I wouldn't be alone again. She was, after all, my best friend, my reason for being here; and despite friendships with Nate, Anneli and Stefan forged from our shared trauma, Sri was like a sister to me. We'd been best friends for 15 years. I nodded, having her there even if she was on the sidelines was a massive comfort to me in those moments.

I'd never know if the strength I got from her leaving me when I was hysterical was also the same solace I got that helped push me through these dark 36 hours and gave me the motivation to keep busy and make myself useful.

I scanned the scene to see who was left and, disheartened, realised there were still a lot of people left to board.

By now, most of the severely injured had boarded and been whisked away to Ampara, the nearest big town with an army hospital. Most of the morning had passed, and the rising sun blistered down on us.

As most of the families were leaving, the surroundings were emptying.

I went back to Nate and Sri, who were both sitting quietly watching. The Squire family was with them.

"Are you OK, Ani?" Nate called, looking over.

"My head's pounding," I replied.

He handed me water, which I gulped down, I felt it snake past my dry, hoarse throat. I'd been shouting so much my throat was raw. I sat down, relieved, taking the weight of my feet for a few moments.

"Are you getting on the next chopper with the Squires, Nate?"

He did not reply.

"Are you going to go with the Squires, Nate? That's the next chopper leaving," I asked again.

"No. I don't want to leave without Fernando," he replied.

"Well, you will have to leave at some point. You can't stay here indefinitely."

"I can't go, because if I leave, he can't find me, and I can't find him."

"Look, it's been over twenty-four hours now. If he was alive, he's probably not here anymore, either. He would have been airlifted to the military hospital."

Nate looked at me, assessing this information, but I could see he didn't want to leave and perhaps give up hope of finding him there at the scene. But he was traumatised, lost his one love, and in the middle of nowhere.

"That's not true. He would never leave me; he would never leave me behind."

"OK, well don't leave yet. There are still a few people to be airlifted. It's just the Squires are due to go next, and I wondered if you were going with them."

"Yeah, I was thinking about it but no."

"Well why don't you come with me, Sri, and Anneli and Stefhan. We're taking the last chopper out," I said hopefully.

I didn't want to lose him at this point. I felt we were kindred spirits and we'd all become dependent on each other.

"I may stay."

"Look, Nate, you're not staying here. I won't permit it; it doesn't make sense. You need to be somewhere you can communicate and contact people. There's nothing here. The water is contaminated, there's no drinking water or food. It's not an option. I'm not leaving without you or leaving anyone here. And if Fernando is still here and alive somewhere and realises that you got on a helicopter to go to a hospital, he will understand and forgive you. You're being ridiculous. It's just not an option, and I'm not leaving without you!"

"OK," Nate said.

I breathed a sigh of relief. I turned to him and gave him a hug.

And so it went. We waited and waited and watched the choppers come and go and airlift people out of there until we couldn't bear it any longer.

Finally, the last of the stragglers were loaded until it was just the five of us left – me, Sri, Anneli, Nate and Stefhan. By now, lunch had long passed. It was late afternoon and as we got the last of the others on board, we eagerly awaited our own transport out.

Many of the Sri Lankans who lived on higher ground were staying; this was their home after all.

Finally, we boarded. The choppers were green and brown camouflage colour, and their big wide doors were open as we all boarded. We took our seats, relieved that finally, after thirty-six hours, we were getting out.

Even though it was only thirty-six hours, it had seemed like several lifetimes. Time stretched out, and we'd lived through so many different moments in horror. It was surreal and unbelievable.

The chopper finally began to lift, the noise deafening. For the first time in a long time I felt a twinge of relief. We were leaving at last.

Our little band of brothers together, four of us who had spent Christmas Day and Eve together, with Nate, our adopted friend.

Friendships forged during a trauma or crisis are formed deep. Those shared days together created an inseparable bond that binds us forever. No one would ever understand the enormity of what we'd been through other than us. This created a link that would transcend time and space, even though we would all carry on with our separate lives afterwards.

As we rose, we could see for the first time the extent of the devastation below us.

EVERYTHING was flat, destroyed, broken for MILES inland. I couldn't make out anything that was familiar. Simply, nothing was left. Where the Galaxy had been, where the lagoon or the bridge had been, there was just simply nothing.

The helicopter ride was another source of fear. The doors remained open as we soared the heights, furthering our fear of survival.

It was incomprehensible this reality of ours so far from normal life hit. Was it possible that just 52 hours before I had been sipping cocktails in the pool at the Hilton?

We all looked haunted, Nate's eyes wide as he also saw what we had survived and contemplated his beloved Fernando lost down there. Would we find him back in Ampara somehow? Had he made it out? I wondered hopefully, but my heart knew it was a long shot.

EIGHTEEN

Ampara

We arrived in Ampara and were set down at the army hospital where we were greeted by the paramedics and whisked off to the wings where we were treated one by one.

Sri left us and rushed straight off to find Wayne.

I sat in a small room while a nurse tended to my wounds in an unceremonious manner. A squirt of iodine on my wounds, she washed my face and squirted iodine on my face and gave me bandages to tie around my legs.

I hobbled over to a small mirror against the wall above the basin.

It was only then that the extent of my wounds was apparent. My face was a mess and swollen, and the pain was really beginning to hit home. As I looked at myself in the mirror, I didn't recognise myself at all.

Mud caked my hair and face and body, and the nurse was slowly sloughing it all off, revealing my soft, bruised, and broken skin underneath.

I didn't have any major injuries though, no broken bones, only superficial injuries that would heal over time. It was the mental scars that would last. The hospital smelt of fear, death, blood, and antiseptic. I needed to get out of those four walls as soon as I was patched up.

I was still wearing the sarong I'd been given. It was filthy, smelly, blood and pus stained, and full of sweat, but it was all I had along with the t-shirt I'd slept in.

I went searching for Sri, perhaps subconsciously knowing that if I stopped, I might collapse, so I pushed on relentlessly, keeping myself busy. This time I was searching for my band of brothers to hold on to something I knew was safe and within reach.

I went from room to room; the hospital was dark and dimly lit with dirty blue and white walls and red concrete floors. I went from room to room, calling, "Sri, Sri?"

Finally, as I turned down another corridor beginning to panic, I heard her voice,

"I'm over here, Ani."

I walked into a ward. On the bed was Wayne with Sri by his side. I felt the shock as I looked at him. His wide smile was gone, and his easy good looks had turned grey with pain. He looked a decade older.

"How is he?"

His face was pale and pained. He looked to be in and out of consciousness, beads of sweat on his forehead dripping down. His tan had all but disappeared as he lay there, wan and limp like a rag doll.

"He's not good. The doctors need to keep him in, so I'm going to stay here with him," she replied.

"How's the baby?" I enquired

"Seems to be OK."

Relieved yet again, I went over and gave her a big hug.

"Ow," she said.

"Oh, sorry," and hurriedly pulled away, forgetting her sore ribs.

"They're giving him antibiotics and painkillers and talking about maybe airlifting him to Colombo but are going to see if he gets any better."

I grabbed her hand.

"He is going to be fine," I told her reassuringly. Her face was stricken with worry.

The hospital was overrun with patients from all over the region as far up as the northeast all the way to the southeast. This was an army hospital, but they had never seen a scene like this and were completely overwhelmed, understaffed, and unknowing of what to do.

Finally, someone took control.

They began calling out for people to gather.

"Right, we have organised accommodation in Ampara," the supervisor said. "We need to clear out those who are not severely injured to make room for more. We will allocate you to the guesthouses in Ampara."

Slowly, they called out names and started to gather people into buses and vans.

Sri backed away.

"What are you going to do, Sri? Stay here tonight?"

"Yes, you go with them, I'll come and find you later. I can't leave him."

She walked back to Wayne, and I was alone again. Panic at being left once more began to rise so I went back in search of Nate, Anneli, and Stefhan, who I'd left to go search for Sri. I spotted them in the crowd and hurried over.

At least there were the four of us there together. I made my way to my band of brothers.

Soon buses began to take able-bodied survivors to the local guesthouses.

"I wish we could get to Colombo," Stefhan said. "This place is not equipped for us all."

"They're making us go on the buses and taking us to some guest houses overnight while they transport people back to Colombo tomorrow," Anneli said to me.

"Yes, I heard," I sighed.

"Why hadn't we been airlifted straight to Colombo? How many more days will this ordeal go on?" Stefhan asked.

Anneli shook her head. She had been a calm constant throughout, never wavering in her demeanour.

"Let's all go together. At least then we'll be in the same guest house," Stefhan said. We all agreed and began making our way out of the hospital to where the buses were taking people away.

"What about Sri?"

"Sri is staying here to be with Wayne. He's not doing very well."

"Is she OK?"

"Yeah, she's just exhausted and in pain. I think she has cracked some ribs, but she can't take anything because of the baby."

Slowly, we made our way to the next bus and waited to be transported. It was dusk by now, and the light blue sky now made way for a darker hue, the mosquitoes were coming out, and the smell of blood and flesh was drawing them to us. Huge tropical insects flew around, and I realised we were going to get eaten alive on top of everything else, which is just what we needed.

The bus filled. Nate and I sat next to each other while Anneli and Stefhan sat behind us. This is how our band would stay for the next few days, Nate and I thrown together in these tragic circumstances. The Squires had left and gone to Colombo.

We arrived at the guesthouse at dark and were given a care package with toothpaste and soap, and we got out to our home for the night. We waited our turn patiently and were allocated a room between two. Everything was free, of course, as we had nothing to pay with – no cards, money, clothes, shoes, nothing.

Nate and I were sharing a room, and Anneli and Stefhan were in the room opposite ours. The room was dark and drab, but we couldn't care less at this point.

Ampara was inland. The tsunami wouldn't be able to get us here; it was almost central Sri Lanka. Our bodies ached for the comfort of a bed and the cleanliness of soap and toothpaste; these little normal things felt like a luxury after what we'd been through.

Exhausted, I plonked myself down on the bed and Nate followed. We lay there lying side by side holding each other in the dimness, no words needed as the enormity of it all began to sink in.

I turned to him.

"Nate. What the fuck just happened?"

We both just stared into the dark, silent.

Finally, we made our way to the bathrooms to have our first shower and wash since the tsunami. We got up to clean up, take a shower, and brush our teeth. I avoided the mirror. I didn't want to look at myself or my ruined face.

As I stood in the shower, I watched the water run brown. The mud that had covered every single person was on me, too, and now it was slowly leaving, in a trickle, down the drain.

We hadn't eaten since the night before since the small scraps of lobster had been offered. Now, finally, our tummies grumbled. We went to the restaurant and some rice and curry were offered; for the first time in a long time we ate. Our appetites were small, the shock and not eating for a day shrinking our appetite and desire for food, but we managed a few morsels and headed back upstairs to the respite of our room.

Nate and I bid goodnight to Anneli and Stefhan as we went back to our rooms.

"Do you think I was right to leave?"

"There was nothing else you could do, Nate. There was no way you could stay there with no water, food, or communication. Besides, I wouldn't have let you because it would have been pointless."

Nate and I started a conversation then that was to play out again and again over the next agonising few days.

"I shouldn't have left him."

"They will send search parties. You did as much as you could. You were going up and down the road, you checked the morgue, you checked where most people were coming up to higher ground, there was nothing else to do there."

"Do you think he's alive, Ani?"

"It's still possible. There are so many different scenarios that could have happened to him, we just don't know."

I was still hopeful and unwilling to admit that anyone I knew had lost someone. But my heart was heavy in case hope turned into dust.

"I feel so guilty."

"Why? You couldn't do any more than you did, Nate."

Nate lowered his voice to a whisper.

"There's something I haven't told you."

"What?"

There was a brief pause, and an anguished look came over his face as his eyes watered up and he turned his head down.

"You know we were together after the first wave, and we were both hanging on to the pole."

"Yes."

"Well, there was another surge of water that lifted us up and separated us for a few seconds. But then he came back, and I felt his hand grabbing on to my shorts. I felt myself beginning to sink with him, and I brushed his hand away. I think he tried to grab my leg, too. That was the last time I saw or felt him again."

Tears slid down his cheeks as he recollected those terrible last moments of contact. I curled around him in comfort.

I paused, imagining this horror. What a terrible thing to carry around.

"There was nothing you could do, Nate. You didn't have a choice; it was completely instinctive and a reflex action of sheer survival. If you hadn't, then you probably wouldn't be here now either. And it's not just you, look at how many parents had to let go of their children's hands to survive, as well as other partners. I'm so sorry this happened to you, but it's not your fault and you did everything you could."

He was quiet.

"Fernando was such a strong swimmer. I was sure he would have made it. He grew up in Brazil on the ocean. He was a surfer. He'd grown up in the Brazilian jungle. If anybody could handle himself, it was Fernando. You know, Ani, he always said he would die before the age of 40. He is 39 now."

"You know, I believe that we die once our soul has fulfilled its purpose here. Maybe he had accomplished what he came here to do and is now gone on to another dimension?" I offered.

"Well, he did always say he wanted a family and a home and that he found that with me," Nate replied.

"Well, there you go then. Maybe that's why he has passed; you gave him what he was looking for. There will always be love there between you."

Nate nodded with tears rolling down his cheeks. I gave him a warm embrace once more and curled up next to him, holding him for comfort.

I understood the power of subliminal messaging even then, and my heart sank when I heard this as I suspected that meant he had gone forever leaving Nate behind.

We shared a lot in those dark hours, our own stories of survival, the horror of the wave. We lay there all night unable to sleep despite our exhaustion, talking through the night, crying, holding on to one another and consoling each other until the morning sun came up once more.

As dawn broke, we headed down for breakfast – what would happen now we asked one another. We looked to see what was happening, was there any news.

Downstairs Anneli and Stefhan were already up.

"Did you sleep?"

"No, you?"

"Not much, I fell asleep for a bit but then woke up with a jump," Stefhan replied.

The horror would keep us sleepless for many nights to come.

We sat around the guesthouse waiting for news, talking to keep us sane when eventually, around mid-morning, a Sri Lankan man came in.

"Is there someone called Ani here?"

"Yes!" I shouted.

"Sri sent me, I'm Nihal."

"A friend of Miss Sri's sent me to find her. I found her at the hospital, and she sent me to find you. Come with me in the jeep. We will go to pick up Sri and Wayne and take you all back to Colombo."

Relief washed over me. I'd been wondering how we were going to get out of there. There was no news about what was going on as it was so chaotic.

"But what about my friends?" I said, pointing at Nate and the Swedes, "I can't leave them."

"They can come, too." All of us breathed a collective sigh of relief.

We grabbed our meagre toiletries and headed to the jeep – the four of us once more on another voyage, this time back to Colombo.

I called Colin.

"Hi, Colin."

"Hi, Ani, is that you?" He replied, recognising my voice immediately.

"Yes, I'm just calling to let you know a friend of ours has sent a car and driver to us and is bringing us back to Colombo. We hope to be there this evening."

"That's great news. You must come to see me when you arrive. Do you have somewhere to stay?"

"I think so. I am getting in touch with a friend of mine, Becky, who I was staying with in Colombo before Christmas to see if we can camp out at hers when we get back."

"Well, come to visit me when you get in. I can send a car if you need," Colin replied.

"Thanks, Colin, hope to see you soon."

NINETEEN

The Long Journey Back to Colombo

We boarded the jeep and bounced off back in the direction of the hospital to collect Sri and Wayne.

The relief was palpable. We had someone come and find us and whisk us away from it all to the relative safety and calm of Colombo, away from this dark, depressing, makeshift hospital in a town not used to seeing many people let alone hordes of injured from the surrounding areas. Facilities were stretched to the max, as hundreds poured in over the hours waiting for inelegant triaging. And that was a polite way of saying it.

Nurses simply doused patients with iodine over sores, blisters, and open wounds. They were rough and rubbed hard, with no sense of care of the trauma people had endured, now having to endure another unsympathetic rite after having survived the worst thing most people couldn't even imagine.

We arrived back at the hospital and got Wayne into the front seat. We were all shocked at his condition and given his size at 6 ft 5 and the injury on his arm, it made sense to have him out at the front. We all noticed a putrid smell emanating from his wound. It was clear his wound was already infected, and it was so bad that the smell made us gag.

He was semi-comatose, flush with fever from the infection in his wound, in and out of consciousness. He lolled, groaning in the front, head rolling from side to side. His normally pale skin was red and blotchy, his blonde, curly hair matted with sweat, dirt and the contents of the ocean still in it. His voice was a mere rasp. It was an unnerving sight, to see a fit, healthy male in his prime now in this feeble state. He was a weak husk of himself and helpless.

We drove away from the dark, dim, depressing hospital, leaving it behind as we started down the windy road.

We continued on the jeep snaking past the winding roads of the Sri Lankan interior. Toothless old ladies smiled at us with their mahogany skin while hanging laundry up by the side of their tin shacks oblivious to the chaos and destruction by the coast. These people were simple villagers. They had little – a tin shack, some rice and dal, and their families – yet they seemed like they didn't have a care in the world, unlike we from the west who had everything and at the same time felt like we had nothing, the void deep inside that so many of us were aligned with.

We stopped at a guest house to refuel, get some food, a bathroom break, and sort out Wayne's wound. We helped Wayne out of the car as he needed assistance to get to a place in the shade and cool where we could dress his wound.

"We can't do this outside, we will need a room," Anneli ordered.

"I'll see if I can get one," I said and headed to the front desk where I spent the next few minutes trying to explain that we needed a room but had no money on us. The receptionist took one look at us and understood we were in the tsunami and kindly arranged a room for us where we escorted Wayne. We took turns freshening up in the bathroom and ordering some food.

I was squeamish at the best of times so I gave Wayne, Sri, Anneli, and Nate a wide berth while they set about cleaning and dressing Wayne's wound. Sri started off by undressing the blood and pus-stained bandage, but before I knew it, she was running out the door gagging.

"Are you OK?" I called out as she came past me, quietly sitting outside.

"I'm going to be sick."

"The wound?"

"Yeah, God, Ani, I am scared for him. It's really bad. I just can't be there. I'm already feeling morning and travel sickness. I just couldn't do it."

"Who's taken over? I enquired.

"Anneli and Nate are undressing the bandage and taking Wayne into the shower to clean it."

"Did you order some food?"

"No, not yet."

"Maybe you need to eat something to settle your stomach after the morning sickness."

"Yes, I do. Can I have a lime juice and some fries please?" she called out to the waiter walking past.

"He said he was going to find some fresh bandages, maybe some flip flops and other things we need."

"Oh, flip flops would be nice!" I exclaimed. I then noticed that we were all still barefoot and in the same clothes we'd gone to bed in on Christmas night. In fact, we were all without a change of clothes, penniless, barefoot, bruised, and cut.

And we settled in for a wait. The sun blistered in the sky, luminous, with a haze of heat shimmering in the air. Blue skies, with flutters of white foam clouds wisped away and the sound of crickets and birds keeping the scene peaceful, a far cry from the destruction we'd left behind.

Nihal came back loaded with supplies, clean bandages, basic painkillers and some other items. Among them were flip flops for all of us!

After a while, Wayne emerged from the room supported by Anneli and Nate, and we all headed back to the jeep keen to get on the road again so we could arrive in Colombo by evening.

We still had no money or anything resembling civilization. Bereft of even the most basic of belongings, we needed to get to Colombo to do everything and anything. We continued bumping our way back, Sri with her morning and travel sickness, Wayne, feverish and infected, but clean for now, Anneli and Stefhan cramped in the back, Nate bereaved and alone, keeping himself quiet.

I was still organising and calling people, making arrangements to get access to Becky's apartment. She had left Sri Lanka and flown out to Edinburgh but said we could stay there. We were to meet some people who had her keys at the building to let us in. One small problem was solved. Only another thousand or so to go. We settled in for the long ride back.

TWENTY

Rag Tails and Cocktails

After a long, hot and dusty trip back to Colombo, we finally arrived on the Galle Road just outside Colombo as it turned night-time. It was 7:00 p.m. but already pitch-black outside.

We were tired but wired from all the adrenaline, lack of sleep, and continuous state of emergency.

Even though it was now only the evening on 28th December, a mere two and half days since we'd nearly died, it felt so much longer. Time stretched out and as we'd been through so many disparate things in such a short space of time, it felt like we'd lived many lifetimes, not just a weekend's equivalent.

The cityscape twinkled in front of us. Cars beeped, while rickshaws careened and swerved around us. Given our brushes with death earlier, this made for a gut wrenching and hair-raising ride. All around us danger loomed, our senses, on high alert, were assaulted by the loud sounds, light, and erratic movements. The world seemed so strange here compared to where we'd come from.

Colombo seemed to be relatively unaffected. They looked like they had gone about their daily business as usual. There was no upside-down cityscape, no broken glass shrouded floor, no smashed houses, or water waist high. No frozen, dead, faces, or shocked people crying hysterically. No, all was relatively "normal" here.

How was it that just hours ago we'd been fighting for our lives and now we were driving into a normal Asian city that looked like nothing had happened at all?

As we arrived, the four of us disembarked at Becky's neighbourhood. Wayne and Sri stayed with the driver, Nihal, so he could take them straight to the best private hospital.

I longed to get into Becky's clean flat and collapse on one of her wide, round, rattan armchairs covered with a huge cushion. The armchair was as much like a hug from a chair that you could get. I'd lain there just a few days before happily chatting with my legs over the arm rests nestled in comfortably.

Now my aching muscles and fatigued body yearned for such comfort, the softness of a bed and armchair allowing a brief respite from the constant pain that throbbed through me.

I unlocked the door and we walked into the flat. It was like a haven. The first thing I did was to immediately put the TV on, switching to BBC news. We were all glued to the screen.

We had only been given snippets and pieces of information and now we were able to get more. Here's what we knew: an earthquake off the coast of Indonesia, the ensuing tsunami that had nearly killed us. We didn't have the details; how many countries had been affected? How many people had been affected and died? We had no real sense of the enormity of it.

We all took up a place either on the chair or on the floor as story upon story was shown. We sat open-mouthed watching the endless coverage. Footage and vox pops constantly streamed on the TV with each piece of news adding to our existing horror, shock, and bewilderment of how we managed to survive when it looked like so many others hadn't.

Here is what we found out. The death count was at 40,000 spanning Indonesia, Sri Lanka, India, Thailand and the Maldives. Most of the dead were from Indonesia followed by Sri Lanka. The earthquake had struck early in the morning, and the first tsunamis hit Banda Ache and the east coast of Sri Lanka where we were.

Snippets of the scale of disaster came through:

"One of the largest earthquakes ever recorded struck off the coast of Indonesia, triggering a tsunami that swept away entire communities around the Indian Ocean."

"The violent upward thrust of the ocean floor displaced billions of tons of seawater, which then raced towards shorelines at terrifying speeds of up to 800 km/h 500 mph radiating across the Indian Ocean from Indonesia to Sri Lanka and beyond."

"Nearly all the victims were taken completely by surprise. There were no adequate warning systems in place, there was no alert issued to people to seek safety."

"Tens of thousands were being reported dead or missing in Sri Lanka and India."

The reportage went on and on.

"So many people died. This is just hard to believe," I said.

We sat long into the night watching in horror.

"I'm arranging to have some money wired over," Nate said. "I should get it tomorrow. We could buy some powdered milk to help the country recover and get some basic items we all need."

"Like clothes and shoes," I said.

We had all called our respective families on arriving in Colombo to let them know we were safe. As I spoke to my mum, she said "I'm getting the next flight over there as soon as I can to be with you."

"No, don't do that Mum. It's a disaster here. The water is contaminated, and they are talking about there being airborne diseases and other diseases that will come because of the water contamination. I am OK. I'm with Sri and Wayne and we are safe now."

Nate was also on the phone updating family and arranging things.

"How is Wayne doing?" I anxiously asked Anneli. "Well, he's in hospital with IV antibiotics, so he should get better," she replied.

"He looked so unwell, though, completely delirious. I hope he makes it through OK. At least the baby will give him some solace and hope at the end," I said, biting the bottom of my lip nervously, worried for his safety. "When shall we go to visit them?"

"Let's get our documents sorted first, then we can head over," Anneli replied.

"Yes, good idea. The hospital is near the embassy, too." In the meantime, I called Sri in the hospital to get an update.

We washed up and got ourselves ready as best we could, then headed downstairs to pick up Sri and walked to Colin's in our muddy clothes and flip flops. We were all quiet, still bedraggled and broken, still in our filthy rags, cut and bruised, with infected wounds and injuries galore.

The five of us looked like zombies from the Michael Jackson *Thriller* video, walking with staccato movements because of broken ribs, bandages, and other scrapes.

We walked up to the imposing gates of the High Commission, as the security guard let us in. A middle-aged, Caucasian man came towards us. He had kind, warm, chestnut eyes and a sympathetic smile on his face as we hobbled over to him.

"Colin?" I spoke. I would recognise him anywhere even though I had never met him except over the phone.

"Ani?" he asked

"Yes," I called out in relief and rushed over to hug him. It was amazing to finally meet the man who had rescued us and had been a lifeline to me with his calm, strong voice amid the chaos.

He ushered us into the living room and gestured towards the long, white, comfortable-looking sofa.

"Please take a seat," he softly spoke as he walked over to the dresser.

Sri and I looked at each other and hesitated, not sure what to do.

"This feels strange," Sri whispered to me.

It was quite ridiculous that we were here at all, standing there fetid, with oozing pus, in this posh diplomat's house, where the sofas were cream and clean.

Sri and I continued looking at the cream sofas and then each other a conspiratorial look in our eyes, the absurdity of the situation brought a twinkle to our eyes.

Sri was still dressed in a multi coloured ra-ra skirt the army base hospital in Ampara had given her. I was still in the same t-shirt I'd been sleeping in and around my waist was the sarong I'd been given by the Sri Lankan woman who took pity on me wandering around half naked post tsunami.

"This feels so odd. Our clothes still carry dead people on them, Sri," I whispered, taking her hand. She knew what I was talking about. We had the day before been sitting on a mat that we later realised was being used to bring dead bodies up from the shore for identification. That had haunted us.

Colin came back into the room.

"What would you all like to drink? How about a cocktail? Gin and tonic? I imagine you could do with a stiff drink." He signaled to his waiting staff.

"Err" – names of cocktails vanished from my mind, "yes that would be lovely," I replied. Yes, that would be lovely, I thought. What an idiotic thing to say.

We were being served cocktails in the High Commissioner's house. In any other time, we'd be dressed in our Sunday best, make up and heels, little black dresses, ready to mix with high society. Nothing could have been less important right then.

The waiter came along with our much-needed drinks and began handing them out to us. We gulped them, warm liquor warming our throats as the alcohol acted like a salve.

He turned to me.

"I just want to say thanks to you all for being so helpful with the rescue effort. You really did some astounding work out there, getting in touch with us via the BBC, tending to the sick, and injured. It can't have been easy after everything you've all been through," Colin remarked.

"We're OK – just really glad to be back here and alive," I replied.

"I can't imagine what you've all been through. We've got reports that the east coast has been flattened for miles inland."

"Yes, it was really big in Arugam Bay. That there were seven deadly tsunamis, and it was the fifth one that took the bridge out leaving us stranded."

"How on earth did you remember the number of the BBC down there?"

I shook my head.

"I honestly have no idea, I left there a few years back! Then the operator refused to put us through until I asked for my old editor."

"Truly amazing work! We have arranged some items for you, just some basics until we can get you more things. Here you go," and Colin handed out a mini care package including a toothbrush and toothpaste and some other toiletries. Then he handed me an envelope before he gave each of us one.

"Here's some money for you so you can get around and get some basics. It's not a lot, but it should be enough for the next couple of days."

We carried on with some chit chat about the scale of the tsunami as we gulped more of our drinks. We spoke about how many British and other tourists looked to be affected and what arrangements were being made to get everyone out of the country.

"It looks like there may be an outbreak of some water borne diseases, which we are trying to get a handle on, so we can react."

"This thing looks really huge, so if you need any help with the rescue effort, coordinating anything, getting on the phone, anything at all, I'd be more than happy to help," I offered,

"Yes, me too," replied Stefhan and Anneli.

"That is very kind of you all," Colin turned to nod at us one by one, kindly, "but we have it covered from here. You can all take a much-needed break now. You've done some fantastic work, and we are very grateful."

Suddenly, it dawned on me that he was seeing us as the casualties of this tragedy. His perspective and the way he interacted with us – kind, caring, paternal – served to remind me and probably the others that in his eyes we were the victims.

I felt my façade beginning to drop and another form of panic begin to take root. I didn't really know who I was if I wasn't taking on the role of the organiser, busying myself with tasks, calling him and the BBC, making lists and registers, administering first aid, organising who had priority on boarding the choppers, etc.

I realised adrenaline had kept me functioning, but looking at Colin's face I knew there was no way he would let us volunteer to help. Now a void would take its place where I would relive the nightmare in the snatches of sleep over the next few months, transporting me back to scene after scene of water crashing over me, drowning me over and over. In my flat in London, on another beach, my sister's home in the USA, no matter that these places were nowhere near the sea I'd wake up drowning in them all.

Would that be my legacy?

TWENTY-ONE

Day 3: A Shopping Spree in Colombo

We all attempted to get some rest that night. I for one was too hyped up to rest properly though, and it would take time for all that adrenaline to leave the system.

As I lay in bed, trying to rest, scenes of devastation and destruction kept infiltrating my mind. Every time I'd close my eyes, I'd be back there reliving the whole terrible experience over and over. I tried curling up next to Nate, and while it provided a modicum of comfort, it was not enough to sleep. I got up early, restless and agitated, with a list of many things to do.

Our first stop was to get some money and some clothes.

Nate had taken on this task with typical American flair. He had access and means and had been on the phone with Oprah's people as soon as he could and had arranged a private search for Fernando.

His people had also immediately arranged for the wire transfer of money, and it was in Colombo waiting to be picked up. It was one less thing for the rest of us to worry about, but phone calls to insurance companies were still to come.

As soon as the banks opened the next morning, the four of us – Nate, me, Stefhan and Anneli – headed there. Sri was staying at the hospital with Wayne; the High Commissioner's driver had dropped her back there the night before.

"Sir, can I help you?" A man came over to us to ask.

"Yes, I'm here to pick up some money that has been wired over to me. I'm Nate Berkus with Oprah Winfrey's people. They have wired across $10,000 US," Nate continued.

"Sir, do you have any identification?"

"No, didn't you hear me? We lost everything in the tsunami. We nearly drowned in Arugam Bay. We have nothing," Nate continued.

"OK, sir, without ID I can't give you such a large sum of money. I understand your situation, but please go to the embassy first and get your new passport ID. We can take care of your request then. We also don't have this amount of rupees available in this branch, so can you go to the main branch in Colombo 1 when you have your passport?"

The bank clerk was kind but clear.

"What do you mean you don't have this amount?" Nate asked incredulously.

"Sir, you're requesting a large sum that we don't have. This is just a local branch. If you go to the main branch, they will have larger sums there. I can inform you of their details and will let them know to expect you," the clerk continued.

This level of bureaucracy further added insult to injury, so we turned around and headed back to the flat. It's difficult to relay how such small tasks became such huge burdens on our already strained systems. When you have nearly lost your life on numerous occasions, nothing has meaning anymore. Things appear to be trivial in relation to these huge cataclysmic events. Getting money, ID, passports were meaningless in the face of death, yet life went on as normal. Where you were changed everything else around you stayed the same. We'd been shaken to the core. Would life ever be the same again having been in the jaws of death so many times? Would these nightmares ever end? What was normal? Such were the questions that bounced around.

TWENTY-TWO

Reality Strikes

Nate was pulling out all the stops to find Fernando, and that afternoon he worked the phones. He spoke with Oprah's people, his family, the security he had employed, all in a bid to find Fernando.

I was just finding what kind of celebrity Nate really was in the US. I didn't realise how big a celebrity Fernando was in his own right. Nate Berkus was an architect and interior designer. He had a regular slot on Oprah doing up people's houses in secret for the show and then doing a big reveal. Fernando was a famous photographer, who had snapped the likes of Naomi Campbell. The two had met a year before and hit it off instantly and had been inseparable ever since. I could see how deeply in love they were.

Eventually, we all sat on the couch and the room fell silent as we turned to the television again. The media coverage was relentless. Every station was broadcasting around the clock. Image after image assailed us. Bodies floating still in the waters. Piles and piles of bodies being carted to makeshift morgues.

Over the coming days and weeks, there would be countless stories relayed on the TV and in newspapers and magazines, stories of guilty grief-stricken parents who had lost children. Stories of loved ones having let their other halves or children's hands go in the fight for survival.

Entire families wiped out.

We sat for long hours simply watching the sheer scale of the disaster on the screen.

Together we understood each other, our collective nightmares, fear, shock, adrenaline, and survival instinct. Each of our individual stories was harrowing, and that afternoon we all sat and shared ours.

Of course, all had a happy ending, except Nate who was facing the reality now of having lost the love of his life.

Not one of us had understood the basic human need for survival until we'd been through it ourselves. It was all about self-preservation, our lizard brains holding on to that desperate need for life. Despite my long depression and malaise with life, when the time had come, I fought tooth and nail to survive. We all had.

But it seemed as if thousands, tens of thousands, had not made it.

"I feel immensely guilty for having been saved where so many families were torn apart," I said, watching yet another shot of photos of small children missing.

"But such is the way of the world; there appears to be no rhyme or reason for those that were taken and those that survived."

"Fernando was such a strong swimmer. That's what I don't understand," Nate said.

We all shook our heads.

Current BBC reports had deaths at close to 40,000. How did we survive and so many people didn't?

This would be a question we would all ask of ourselves in our quiet moments, again and again.

There we were the four of us, these new friends and bonds I'd formed. It was a strange paradox as at the same time Sri was more distant, as she was at the hospital with Wayne the entire time and stayed with him. It was not surprising. Amongst the backdrop of this huge disaster, relationships were formed and tested.

It was impossible to process all these emotions and feelings at the time, so the four of us clung to each other as our trauma family. We had barely left each other's sides since we'd all been united on the hill after the first few waves on our way to higher ground.

TWENTY-THREE

Documents and Papers

Stefhan and Anneli had been on the phone to the Swedish Embassy, and we got the news that they were arranging a car to pick them up. As the four of us were now inseparable, Nate and I decided to go with them. We couldn't leave each other; we were each other's security blanket. When the four of us were together, we felt stronger, not as alone, even though we were all alone really.

It seemed the most alone was Nate who was still searching for Fernando. While we were moving forward with getting our documents – he was facing the real truth that Fernando did not make it. This was a truth we all knew was looming, and we no longer tried to keep up the positive outlook.

Suddenly, the bell from security rang in the flat and a big, red, Volvo Jeep turned up downstairs to take us to the Swedish Embassy. The embassy looked more like a big, beautiful house than anything official. The driveway was a curve around the building, and we all looked at the curiously, calm building set in a garden in the middle of a normally chaotic city.

The Swedish government didn't have as large a presence as the British in Sri Lanka, and this meant the building was relatively empty. We were greeted warmly by the staff ushering us inside the big, cool, clean interior of the embassy.

Drinks were offered, and we immediately felt a sense of calm, control, and order in that building that signified all things Swede from the modern, clean, minimalist Scandi furniture, the light-coloured whitewashed walls, and the pale wood desks and chairs.

Someone gave each of us a care pack, which consisted of more toiletries. This one had a t-shirt and a hat. They were much better organised here, and I could finally put on a fresh t-shirt.

We waited while Stefhan and Anneli were able to get pictures taken for their new passports. Not temporary passports either, but real ones.

Colin had already informed me the night before that Sri and I wouldn't be able to get passports to travel due to the sheer volume of British tourists on holiday there, and so we'd be issued with a formal letter of travel instead, which would act like a temporary passport.

We still had no plans to leave though. We were in limbo but with a purpose to stay and help out the country.

We left the embassy, encouraged by the ease of the process, and another plan was formed.

We would all head to our respective embassies, me to the British High Commission main building and Nate to the

US Embassy. Once we were done, we would meet after to go to the bank to pick up the money Nate had arranged.

The British High Commission was bedlam. British people were the number one tourist country to visit Sri Lanka in those days, and there was also a large expat community. Hundreds of people spilled out of the building. There was a huge queue, and my heart sank as I realised it could be hours before I got out of there.

I took my number in the queue and settled in for a long wait.

The TV was on in the waiting room on BBC 24-hour TV news, and I sat and watched with my eyes glued. The death toll was climbing over 40,000 people.

Of course, we'd find out months later the death toll was six times that amount, nearing a quarter of a million people. But already at 40,000 it was an unprecedented amount of people to perish in one catastrophic event.

The frailty of human life and of our existence became ever more apparent and fear hit me again. If that many souls could be wiped out within seconds on Earth, it was easy to see how a species could be eliminated from a bigger disaster like a meteor. My horror and amazement were both activated in equal proportions, bringing new meaning to the duality of life and the comedy and tragedy that affects us all.

Colin spied me in the waiting room and called out to me. "You should have let me know you were here," he exclaimed.

"Oh, I didn't want to bother you. You must be so busy."

"Not too busy for you," he smiled kindly and ushered me into his office where he sorted out my paperwork for me.

I headed back to Becky' s where we all reunited with our travel documents and new ID. We headed to the bank once more, but this time to the main head office.

"How was the US embassy, Nate?"

"Awful," he replied.

"Why?" I asked.

"They were so disorganised compared to the Swedish embassy, though they were expecting me as Colin Powell's people and Oprah had contacted them. They met me as soon as I arrived, so that helped."

"Well, that must have sped it up."

"Ani, it was terrible. There were all these children on their own, crying. They wanted to take me to the front, but there was no way I was going to do that. All these kids had lost their parents."

I stood speechless.

"Oh, that really brings it home. I am an adult and struggling. I can't even imagine the plight of those poor kids."

It was horrendous. They also had no equipment. They didn't even have the facilities there to take my picture at the embassy. The US embassy, the world's greatest superpower, and they didn't have a place to take passport photos. Nothing like the Swedish embassy at all."

Nate was angry, and it was the first time I had seen him lose his cool. His general nature was so sweet that this was his first outburst.

"So where did you go?" Anneli asked.

"There was a place across the road I had to go to." Nate's face was flushed with anger. I wasn't surprised, seeing those children must have been truly horrendous.

"I called my mom again, and she was so relieved. Everyone is worried sick, and it is all over the news back home. The whole world is in shock, she said."

Just then the phone rang. It was for Nate, and it was from the Singapore rescue team looking for Fernando. He chatted for just a second.

"No news. They still haven't found Fernando," he sat down on the couch. "I feel so guilty sending out a search party spending thousands of dollars when there are so many other people missing."

I sat next to him.

"Nate it's lucky you have the means to be able to do this. Isn't that what having access to money is about? Being able to use it in your hour of need?" I tried to comfort him.

"Yes, I suppose. It's just I know I won't be able to rest until I've done everything I can to find him."

"Exactly, hopefully they will find him," I offered up in a thin voice, secretly wondering if after three days they really would

TWENTY-FOUR

Bags of Money

With Nate's new passport, we all headed out to the bank to get the money. Sri was still in the hospital with Wayne, so once more we went, the four of us, and on the way back we were going to go to the hospital to check in on the two of them.

On arrival at the bank, Nate made himself known.

"Hi, I'm Nate Berkus. I was in the tsunami and have had some money wired across, $10,000, to pick up. I was told by the other branch to come here with my new passport to get the money."

"Yes, sir, we've been expecting you. Sorry to hear of your unfortunate circumstances. Please come this way."

The bank manager led us to his office where he motioned for us all to sit down.

"Would you like a drink? Some water? Tea or coffee?"

"Some coffee would be great."

The bank manager got on the phone to order the coffees and set about inputting Nate's details to release the money.

"Do you have some bags to take the money?" he enquired.

I looked at him and raised an eyebrow.

"Bags?"

"No, we don't have anything," Nate replied.

"OK, we will arrange some bags for you."

As he was speaking, a huge pallet was wheeled in with wads of cash on it.

We all stared incredulously. I'd forgotten that here the currency was so devalued that $10,000 in rupees would be a much larger amount to carry. There was no way we'd get all this cash into bags, I thought. The staff arrived with some carrier bags, and we all began stuffing the cash into the bags, filling them to the brim and then filling them some more.

"This is ridiculous," I said. But we kept stuffing.

Eventually, all the money was in the bags and Nate had signed all the necessary paperwork. The manager enquired as to how we were going to get home and if we had a reliable driver.

As we didn't, he rushed to call a cab.

"I don't think a rickshaw is right for today," he smiled as he ushered us into the closed car and firmly shut the door.

We all burst into laughter, the absurdity of the last hour having us in fits of giggles. This had taken the crazy to the next level.

We hugged the money to our chests as we went back to the flat to drop off some of the bags, and then we headed out to the large shopping mall in the city centre.

At that stage, we still only had the clothes on our back, with the new T-shirts from the Swedish embassy. We went to one of the few multi-story shopping malls in Colombo, the House of Fashion, and continued our weary journey.

We arrived at the huge department store. It was like a world removed. This was such an antithesis from everything we'd been through my brain really couldn't compute. We all wandered around listlessly, confused and weak. I stared straight through at things as we walked around like zombies. Christmas songs played in the store as holiday decorations still adorned the department store and people were shopping the sales.

"Buy anything you want or need," Nate said. "I'm picking up the tab so don't worry. Get whatever you want." I stared at the Christmas ribbons. The department store was decorated garishly for Christmas with brightly-coloured tinsel and the kitschness that epitomised traditional Sri Lankan taste.

Christmas Sale! – every shop promised, and tinny Christmas carols blared over the cheap sound system. I noticed dozens of Sri Lankans all staring at us and the state we were in, pointing and whispering.

I didn't know what I needed or wanted, probably some underwear would be good. I'd been knickerless for days now. I threw a new skirt and dress in and some tops. I definitely needed a handbag to put my items into as well as a larger bag for any clothes I'd buy.

I saw a brightly coloured orange handbag that caught my eye. Orange was my favourite colour, and this bag had the advantage of being a mini backpack, so I added that to my basket.

I tried a few dresses on.

"What do you think of this, Nate?" I asked him from the changing rooms, with one of the dresses I'd picked up.

He did a double-take.

"God no, Ani. You look like a hooker in that. Take it off!"

I cracked up laughing. The tsunami may have taken away my dress sense, but it hadn't totally dented my sense of humour.

"Let me try something else on."

All around us the local people stared. In a country where staring was the norm, they stared even harder, curious at our disheveled state.

As we stood in the queue, the lady on the checkout looked at us.

"I'd like to take this, but I'd like to wear it out. Is that OK?"

"Where were you?" she asked.

"Arugam Bay," replied Nate.

Her eyes widened and she bent down under the counter and started bringing out samples of creams and moisturisers and other free sample stuff.

Nate's eyes began to water again as he was taken aback by the kindness of the lady.

As she continued to ring up our items, I noticed the amount jumped suddenly after inputting my orange handbag. I peered at the amount and wondered why it was so expensive and noticed the little LV in the corner of the bag. I'd picked up a Louis Vuitton handbag without realising it.

The juxtaposition of having lost all our material possessions, safety, dignity, security in life, and now we were buying designer handbags when we had lost everything that meant something to us was an irony not lost upon me.

We still had virtually no sleep for days on end; our bodies throbbed with pain. I didn't realise at the time, but all my wounds had become infected with the tropical heat, and my head felt full of cotton wool, like I'd had a lobotomy or the closest I could assume a lobotomy felt like.

As we left the store laden with bags and bags worth of stuff, Nate turned round to me.

"Wasn't that lady so kind?" Tears glistened in his eyes.

"Why?" I replied.

"For giving us all that stuff for free, the creams, and lotions."

I looked at him curiously.

"They were only samples, Nate," I said, a bit puzzled by his reaction.

"I know, but it was so nice of her."

"I suppose, but it's kind of the least she could do given we've all survived a tsunami and spent thousands of dollars in there, no?" I replied with an eyebrow raised.

We both burst out laughing. Nate at my cynicism, me at his over-emotional reaction to a few free toiletry samples. We doubled over in laughter, hysterically laughing and crying simultaneously. A moment of lightness showing how the comedy and tragedy of life were inexplicably intertwined, the duality of life once more.

Next, we stopped at the shop to buy milk powder. Hundreds of packets of milk powder to distribute to families affected by the tsunami. It was one of the main staples volunteers were distributing to those affected. We donated them to our friend's charity, Giles who had sent Nihal to pick us up. He had mobilised around the island quickly and effectively due to his extensive contacts on the island.

Dead bodies and rotting animals had contaminated the food chain around the coast, and you didn't know how long it would take to get aid to the affected areas. Places like Arugam Bay and other villages on the east coast were hard-to-reach areas in the first place let alone after seven tsunamis hit the shores flattening everything in sight for miles inland.

We lugged bags full of milk powder up to the flat and collapsed once more. Colombo was a hot, dusty, humid city, busy with traffic and constant sound and movement. Our nerves were exposed and raw, and it had taken monumental effort to go round the city that day and navigate embassies, money, and shopping all in one day.

The back of my eyelids felt sucked of all moisture, drained, my eye twitching from sleeplessness and nerves and fatigue seeped deep into my bones. I felt heavy-limbed and woolen-headed. We were mere shadows of ourselves, going through the motions to stay alive and navigate our way through usually normal tasks, which now felt like climbing Mount Everest at every turn.

The TV was switched on to the 24-hour news coverage of the BBC. The tsunami was everywhere and dominated the news schedule. Blanket wall-to-wall coverage everywhere and every angle on the disaster. Scientific data was poured over, images of gruesome deaths and bodies, footage from tourists taken that showed people getting swept up in the disaster. There were scenes of people, trucks, and cars being washed away with the wave and the might of the ocean tearing down buildings. It was a news bonanza.

The sheer facts surrounding the tsunami were ever more astounding.

"The energy released by the earthquake on the Earth's surface was the equivalent to 1500 times that of the Hiroshima atom bomb. It was the third largest earthquake recorded ever in history."

"We lost microseconds of our day such was the huge impact that the earth wobbled on its axis by an inch."

Various experts were brought in to fill in the gaps and trotted out facts one by one. We sat glued to the coverage, some of us dozing off right there and then for a few snatched seconds or minutes at a time before our heads would snap back.

TWENTY-FIVE

Day 4: New Year's Eve and a Hasty Retreat

Dawn broke on 30th December, and it had been only four days since the tsunami had struck.

Wayne had not left the hospital since the day we had arrived, and Sri had spent all of her time there with him. As they lived in Sri Lanka, they hadn't had the same urgency around getting passports and IDs sorted, unlike the rest of us.

We'd been visiting Wayne in hospital daily, usually in the evenings, and yet he still was unwell. We were also going today.

This hospital was big and clean, with shiny floors and a large entranceway, a world apart from the military one at Ampara. He was in a private room, and Sri had a cot bed in the room with him.

I'd first met Sri at uni. We'd both flunked our A levels despite both being cited as Oxbridge candidates by our colleges, and we failed our exams for different reasons. Sri had lost her dad just before her exams from a sudden heart attack, and I had gotten a taste of freedom as a teenager and was more interested in expressing that freedom than studying.

The upshot of this had been that we'd both ended up on the same course at UWE.

She seemed like an ominous figure, sitting in the back of the lecture hall. Back then she had short-cropped hair, shaved at the bottom and sides wearing camouflage dungarees and Doc Marten boots. She looked fearsome in her punk style and shaven head. I'd never seen another Asian girl dress like that or wear their hair that way, and I was fascinated by her instantly but too scared to approach her at first. Ironic as apparently I was the scary one. I later realised that she was nothing like her look, rather a very kind, warm, person underneath it, but this was her expression at her father's untimely demise.

She looked tired but resilient as she stayed by Wayne's bed.

Wayne was still fighting his infections. He had originally sustained a gash of over 25 cm long in his bicep – luckily just missing key arteries. They had stitched him up in Ampara but without cleaning out the wound properly. That was the smell we had on our trip back to Colombo. It was his arm going septic. When we got to Colombo and admitted him to one of the best private hospitals, they had immediately unstitched the wound, triaged it again, and left it open to heal as it was so infected. He was on IV antibiotics and would remain so for a further four months. It was only when he arrived back to Australia a few weeks later for better medical attention did they identify a further infection that came from one of his cuts on the leg.

These kinds of deadly infections were to kill many survivors.

After we checked in to see how he was and caught up with Sri, we headed out to the cafeteria. We hadn't eaten yet that day, and our tummies were rumbling. Dishes of local rice and curry lined up to one side, and the place was filled with staff and visitors alike. Most of them tucked into the food in the traditional way this part of the world did, eating with their hands.

"What shall we get?" I turned to Nate and asked.

"Are you kidding me? I'm not eating that," Nate grimaced.

"What do you mean?" I turned to look at him and as he made a disapproving face.

"I'm not eating that. It looks disgusting."

"What do you mean it's disgusting? We haven't eaten properly for days, and we should eat a proper meal."

"Yes, but not here. They're all eating with their hands. No way."

I stared at him aghast.

"Nate, you can't say that!" I admonished.

"Why?"

"Because much of the world's population eat with their hands. Most of the Indian subcontinent and other parts of the world, too. You can't say that!"

He looked suitably chastised.

"Sorry, Ani. It's my first time in Asia to be honest. Fernando dragged me here. I'm not used to it, and the food and the way they're eating looks dirty to me."

We looked at each other, and the look on his face of sheer horror made me burst out laughing and he joined in.

"I can't believe you think this is so gross after what we've been through in the tsunami, but OK, let's go. Let's find ourselves something and somewhere nicer to eat."

And arm in arm we headed back out of the cafeteria and up to the room to tell the others what we were up to.

"Sri, we're going to head out to eat. Do you want to come?"

"Yes."

We headed to one of Colombo's hippest and nicest restaurants, Gallery Café.

As we entered, a small rectangular pond of water greeted us. We walked through a mahogany corridor adorned with fine art photos on the walls, leading to the bar area with comfortable suede sofas and armchairs. Passing through the outdoor restaurant with its water feature and dark coloured tables and chairs, we followed the waiter to our table.

After we'd eaten, we headed back to Becky's to rest. It had been a non-stop week of activity, and none of us had really had time to let things sink in. We'd all been preoccupied with surviving until now, so we were finally beginning to let our guard down and relax a little.

We plonked ourselves back down on the circular rattan armchairs at Becky's. Sri headed back to the hospital, so it was Nate and I and the Swedish couple on our own again, and as usual we switched on BBC news as we did every day.

Nate turned to me.

"Ani, I think he's gone."

I looked at him, confused for a second. Then it dawned.

"I spoke to Mom and the security guys last night."

"What did they say?"

"Still no sign of him. They've searched the whole area but can't find him. They have been to every hospital and every morgue. Nothing. He's not coming back, is he Ani?" His head hung low, eyes like oceans full of pain and lost love, shoulders slumped, as the enormity of what he voiced out loud was a huge weight on his shoulders.

I bit my lip. Until now I had always reassured Nate that Fernando could still be found, but I'd had my suspicions for a while now that he might not come back to him. My sense of movie happiness made me desperately want for Nate's sake for him to be found so our little band of brothers could remain intact.

"I don't think so, babe," I reached over to him to envelop him in a hug as tears began to roll down his face.

There were no words I could say that would make his grief go away. But now at least he could begin the long, windy road to accept that he may be dead.

"I had to send the search party in. I had to know I did everything I could."

"Of course, you did. You'd have never forgiven yourself if you hadn't."

His face was wet.

"You did everything you could," I repeated, but nothing I said could make any difference.

"I can't sleep, Ani. Every time I close my eyes, his face is there."

I nodded and the two of us sat there for a while. There was truly nothing to say and for once my "I can fix anything" armour just fell flat. I could not fix this at all.

Suddenly an update came onto the screen.

BREAKING NEWS!

"We're getting reports of an aftershock being reported in India that could trigger another tsunami," the reporter announced. My ears pricked up.

"Quick, guys, come listen to this," I called out to the others.

"Sounds like they're saying there's the possibility of another tsunami to hit India and Sri Lanka."

Suddenly, we were all listening intently. My heart started to race as once more we were no longer safe, and our life was under threat.

The news report continued.

"The tsunami that hit on 26th December, 2004, looks to have moved the earth's crust by millimetres, exposing cracks and creating more instability. It is thought that an aftershock may hit India in the next few days triggering another potential tsunami in the region. Emergency services are already stretched to the limit. Another tsunami would hamper the already limited resources in the area. Billions of dollars of aid and donations have been pouring into the region during the aftermath of this huge catastrophe."

I turned to look at Nate.

"What are we going to do?" I asked.

All logic escaped us. It didn't matter that we were in the main city of Colombo and safe.

We didn't want to stay in the country anymore to help out if there was the danger of having to go through what we went through already. That was too much for any of us to bear. And we all jumped up busying ourselves, shouting at each other, and general bedlam ensued. We were still using the phone Colin had given us to call our friends and family.

"I'll make a call to my dad to get us flights out of here." Nate was already on the phone dialing the USA.

"I'll call Becky to see if she can get us a flight, too!" I replied. We gathered around in terror, rushing around the flat gathering our things.

"Hey, Dad, we need to get out of here. Can you get us some flights out to London, Stockholm and Chicago. There are four of us, two to Stockholm, one to London."

We all waited with bated breath.

"No, we all need to travel together. I can't leave them behind."

Nate's dad continued to talk on the other end as we all listened till he finally got off the phone.

"He'll call me back as soon as he's arranged it."

An hour later the phone rang. Nate turned to us.

"He's booked us flights out tomorrow evening, first class with Jordan Air. We're leaving around 7:00 p.m. They were the earliest flights he could find. All the flights have been booked out due to everyone else leaving the country."

It was already evening time, so we only had twenty-four hours before we would finally leave this place. We headed to the hospital to say our goodbyes to Sri and Wayne. I tried to convince them to come, but Wayne's condition was so bad there was no way he could leave, and of course, Sri had to stay by his side.

I felt bad deserting her, but she reassured me they would be fine. This was their home after all, and they would be safe where they were.

I called Jo, my flatmate, to tell her I would be arriving and to let me in as I was without my door keys.

The entire next day was a blur. We were glued to BBC TV news for more information on the impending second tsunami. We stayed in the apartment, which was relatively safe far from the ocean on the fourth floor.

Until finally it was time to leave for the airport.

We headed to the airport, surveying our last few hours in the country that had wreaked havoc in our lives. As we drove up, I realised it was New Year's Eve and it was just seven days since I had landed there on the 23rd December. As we made our way through security, we were quietly contemplative as we were finally leaving. We made our way through with no problems, breathing a sigh of relief as we entered the departures concourse one step closer to freedom.

We sat down in the cool air-conditioned lounge. We were all sharing the plane until we reached London where Anneli and Stefhan and Nate would leave me to go to their respective homes, We would be a family no more and would be separated for the first time since disaster struck.

It was a strange feeling to leave these people that I'd spent almost every moment with over the past week. We'd gained so much comfort being with each other in those days, becoming friends, supporting each other. We had all become dependent on each other. It would be very weird to now be separated. The bond that you share with people who have experienced the same thing as you is not easily broken. No one would know other than them how terrifying our ordeal had really been. How we'd lean on each other for comfort and support and how bereft and alone we would feel once we arrived back to our familiar homes. Nothing would ever be the same again after this seismic event shook even the Earth off its axis.

Finally, it was time to board. Our flight would be transiting via Amman airport, as the only direct flights to Sri Lanka were with their home carrier, Sri Lankan Airlines. Everyone else had to pass through their airport hubs before carrying us on to London.

We boarded turning left at the door, which was a welcome reprieve, economy looked very full and there were just us four in the first class seats.

Nate and I sat next to each other, and Anneli and Stefhan sat across the aisle from us. I rested my head on Nate's shoulder.

We arrived in Amman, Jordan, around midnight. It was now 2005 and we had spent our New Year's Eve on a plane, not even noticing that it was a New Year, and we were one more step closer to home.

We had to make our way through transit and disembarked the plane where we had to go through two sets of security to another terminal to catch our second plane, which would take us to London.

The concourse was sparse, a far cry from the busyness of Colombo airport, and we queued to go through security for our flight.

As the other three headed out in front, I was last, and Nate waited for me on the other side of the metal detector screener. I showed the tall, Jordanian security passport controller my letter.

"Passport," he said.

"This is my letter to travel," I replied. He looked at me blankly, not understanding.

"Passport," he repeated.

"This is my passport; I was in the tsunami in Sri Lanka. This is a document for travel."

The security guard looked at me blankly and again repeated, "Passport."

"I don't have a passport! I was in the tsunami in Sri Lanka. I lost everything. This is from the British High Commissio,." I said, pointing to the letterhead. "This is sufficient to travel with."

The doors to the aircraft were beginning to close, and Nate called out to them, "Wait! What's going on, Ani?"

"He won't let me through. He keeps asking for a passport."

Exasperated, my blood pressure began to rise as I panicked that I might be left in this no man's land of Amman terminal without anyone to help me.

"Let her through," Nate called out in an authoritative voice.

"No, she doesn't have a passport. She can't travel."

My heart sank, I tried to mime why I didn't have a passport and before we knew it Nate and I were both acting out drowning, arms up flailing around, head going under, unable to breathe, miming rolling around and pointing to our injuries.

"Tsunami! Sri Lanka!" I cried. Then I mimed a huge wave coming across, and once more I was acting as though I was underwater. I pointed to all my cuts and bruises and bandages, and once more mimed being hit and knocked around. It was a hilarious sight to look at in hindsight, and if I hadn't been so tense, I would have been laughing hysterically.

The other guards were also looking on in amused puzzlement. "What were these crazy people doing?" they probably thought. As Nate joined in, "We've been in the tsunami, in Sri Lanka. We lost all our stuff. This is a letter for her to travel issued by the High Commission."

"Let her come, we're not leaving without her." His voice rose, and for the second time I saw him getting angry and was so grateful for his support in those moments. I wasn't sure whether they would board without me and leave me there, so his words of encouragement gave me the solace I needed to know I wasn't going to be abandoned at the terminal.

Finally, one of the other security guards said something in Arabic to his colleague and it seemed like the penny dropped.

"Ah, tsunami?" He turned round to me and asked his eyes widening as suddenly all the clues were coming to place.

"Yes, yes, yes, tsunami!"

He looked at my injuries once more and saw my injured face, noted the bandages on all of us, blood and pus seeping through giving a yellowish red stain to them and decided that probably yes, we had been in a tsunami, and this was enough proof.

Finally, they let me pass.

TWENTY-SIX

Home

I got out of the taxi and rang the doorbell and waited for my flatmate to let me in.

The hall light came on from the top entrance to my home as I peered up, hoping she had stayed up for me.

It had only been ten days since I'd left here for my adventures in the sun. Full of hope, joy with the possibilities of this new dream life I was about to create. And now it had all come tumbling down like a Jenga game.

I felt like a Jenga game myself, and that one crucial piece that holds everything together had been ripped away from me and left me collapsed in a heap just like those wooden blocks ended up.

Jo raced down the stairs and let me in. She gave me a warm hug without saying anything. Her eyes said it all as they were full of empathy and sorrow for the state I was in.

I walked into my living room and stared. Everything was neat, in its place, red and gold picture frames on the shelves, the tall floor lamps with orange shades, my big bottle green vase given to me as a birthday gift filled with flowers, the alabaster painted bookshelf. My coffee table, made from half of a tree trunk. The jewel-coloured silk embroidered cushions adorned the sofa creating warmth and comfort.

Everything was in order, carefully placed and in their perfect position, and it just didn't make any sense. It blew my mind.

Everything looked so normal and yet life had taken a sudden dark and twisty turn.

Chaos had become my new world order, and I was having trouble adjusting to the place I had called home for five years.

How is it that a ten-day experience can overlay everything else in your life?

I was anxious to have a proper bath in my own home with clean laundered clothes that didn't smell of death and to warm my bones from the biting cold outside.

Jo was busy making cups of tea, or in my case a stiff drink, getting towels and asking after my every need. I sank into the warmth of the bath, the soapy bubbles frothed around me, enveloping me in their light embrace, and finally I was home. I lay there staring at the mosaic coffee-coloured titles that bordered the bathroom while slugging my JD and coke, the lights on dim as I allowed the heat of the water to wash away my woes.

I dozed off for a second only to awake shrieking as the familiar images and sensations of being under water would haunt me for many years to come.

Before I knew it Jo was there helping me out of the bath. She took me to bed and asked what I needed.

That night sleep eluded me despite the exhaustion. I was too scared of the images that came when I closed my eyes. So later in the night I got up, left my bed, and went to lay on the sofa in the lounge instead with the TV on in the hope that the distraction of a movie would eliminate those scenes from my eyes. I would doze off intermittently only to wake up sweating with cold fear once again.

TWENTY-SEVEN

London Adjustment

The next few days were a blur.

Mum arrived from Pakistan where my sister and her had been on a shopping trip for my sister's upcoming nuptials. One of the ceremonies was supposed to have been in Pakistan, and I was meant to have joined them there after Sri Lanka.

My dad had been watching the news and asked her, "Isn't Anila in that area in Sri Lanka?" Mum had turned around abruptly and said yes and then had been frantically trying to call me, Sri, the hotel, and friends and family in London to see if they had heard from us.

When she had finally spoken to me, she had been frantic with worry and was about to head straight to Colombo when I had told her not to due to the state of the country post disaster. Instead she had booked a flight to London to come and take care of me on my return.

Dad had named me Anila; I'd hated my name growing up. I was a target for bullies already, but with my name it was even worse. Along with "Paki," I was called "Anilla vanilla." My name was pronounced the same as Anita but with an l instead. People would pronounce it like vanilla along with annihilator, which is why I switched it to Ani.

Mum had flown back to look after me as soon as she could. She was worried sick; I'd managed to speak to her once we'd arrived in Colombo, but she didn't really understand the extent of what I'd been through until she saw me and witnessed for herself how terrified and jumpy I was.

Her eyes filled with tears as she contemplated my state whilst simultaneously brushing it to one side as she fussed over me like a mother hen.

Friends started to visit. Slowly to begin with and then more steadily. Some friends came round insisting we'd go out for cocktails at the weekend while I looked at them like they'd gone mad. If you could get me out the house it would have been a big enough deal let alone get me to a cocktail bar. This kind of statement was an indication of how no one could come close to imagining what it had been like in those dark hours and days.

I spent those first few days catatonic. Now that I was home, all that rage, fury, and anger that had kept me going at the scene and in Colombo, keeping the shock and hysteria at bay, now turned inward and a huge black cloud descended and engulfed me in its arms holding me tight, suffocating me with its inky heaviness.

I drank too many JDs and coke.

Sleep escaped me, as I had been asleep when the tsunami hit. My sleep was one of the most affected things. I'd wake up screaming and couldn't be left alone for a minute; mum and friends took turns spending time with me as I woke up to swirls of waves washing over me time and time again for a few moments. I'd manage to drift off here and there.

Jo was amazing. She didn't care about the suitcase as it turned out. Somewhere in my mind, I knew it didn't matter, but shock had meant I had an extraordinary reaction to finding any things of mine and I had grown weirdly attached to things I'd found in the debris even though I'd been ordered by Sri to leave them there.

Jo was the perfect flatmate. She worked as a children's home manager so came from a social care background and set her management and organisational skills to work finding out about therapists specialising in trauma therapy in my local area.

All this activity happened around me, but I didn't really know what was going on.

I was barely speaking, eating, or sleeping. I'd go to sleep drinking JD and cokes to switch off and numb myself to stop the constant horror movie in front of my eyes.

When I'd wake up, my hand would reach for the drink by the side of the bed, and I'd continue the same process.

My mom watched with wide eyes.

"Beta, it's OK, you're safe now. I am here. You're safe." Under her breath, she would be constantly muttering a prayer to Allah to relieve me from suffering and calling on protection. Nobody knew what to do. She'd been on 24/7 watch since she'd arrived, taking care of me and staying with me. She was exhausted, too.

One evening some friends had come to visit, I was lying on the wide, comfy sofa resting half awake, half sleeping. There were two friends there at the time.

They were chatting amongst themselves while I drifted in between consciousness and sleep. Suddenly, the Velux window clattered on the side from a large gust of wind causing a sudden, unexpected bang, and I awoke from my light sleep screaming.

This wild animal scream came out of me.

I'd never heard anything as scary before. It was like a crazed, wounded animal. I realised that it was me making that sound. But I could not stop.

I screamed at the top of my voice, completely losing my mind and behaving like cornered prey.

My two friends were shocked. They didn't know what to do. They couldn't do anything to appease me. I had curled up into a foetal position, and those screams were pure animalistic screams, as the terror of the mere thought of another tsunami triggered a huge response. I'm sure the whole neighbourhood would have heard me even though we were in the loft. Suddenly, my mum ran up the stairs and burst in.

"What happened?" she shouted.

She had been trying to get a few minutes of rest now that I was with some friends.

"She was asleep on the sofa and then the wind blew the window a bit and it made a small noise and then she started screaming."

"Anila, Anila, it's OK, beta. You're safe now." My mum tried to soothe me. But I was still screaming hysterically.

My friends didn't know what to do. I bet they didn't think going for cocktails was a good idea anymore. But I simply could not stop.

Eventually, after what seemed an eternity. I broke into guttural sobs.

My senses were on such high alert, every fibre of my being standing to attention, including the hairs on the back of my neck. My hearing was finely tuned, and I could hear the slightest noise barely discernible. I would hear the rustle of a leaf from a hundred metres away.

It was the effect of all the adrenaline and the body's natural animal instinct to keep you alive that created all these new experiences and it was exhausting.

Imagine every single cell in your body on extreme alarm alert twenty-four seven. It's impossible, you can't, but that's how it was for me in those days and weeks in the aftermath of the world's biggest disaster.

Each day I would be updated via the news of the death toll, and each day it seemed to multiply. 40,000 became 80,000, which then became 120,000, and it kept going up, up, up. With each multiplication there was more amazement at how I'd survived, coupled with the crushing guilt I felt.

I'd lost most of my things in the tsunami, my favourite clothes, music and PJs.

TWENTY-EIGHT

The Oprah Show Calls

On arrival back to London Jo had arranged for doctors' appointments and check-ups to make sure I was OK. The doctor ran a full blood work as well as other diagnostics to find I had a few different strains of food poisoning from ingesting the contaminated water- campylobacter and hyper pylori to name a couple. Added to that my wounds *had* gotten infected, so I was given a course of strong antibiotics. Jo had made sure I had gone to get checked out by the doctors as soon as possible. I was such a zombie that her no nonsense, take care of everything skills were a godsend at that time. Left to my own devices I'd have drunk myself into a stupor and tried to bury my head in the sand.

She started making enquiries about a trauma therapist specialising in such cases and made appointments for assessments and accompanied me to my first appointment.

I'd called work. Obviously they'd seen the news and were worried sick about me, relieved that I was alive after what they'd seen on the TV they were sure I'd perished. My manager had been really kind and sweet. I heard the quaver in his voice and could almost see the tears in his eyes as he reassured me, "Take all the time you need Ani, we're just glad you're alive. If there's anything you need or anything we can do for you, please do ask."

Considering I was a contractor and he didn't really owe me anything it was nice to be soothed and reassured I had my job if and when I wanted it. Right now it was the furthest thing from my mind. I could barely speak let alone contemplate work again. Plus, it all seemed so meaningless after what I had been through and witnessed.

Almost a week after I got home, I got a call from Nate.

My heart leapt as I heard his voice.

"I'm home now, isn't it weird being back?"

"I know, right. How are you managing?"

"My mum and dad were waiting at my home when I got back and had been there for days wondering when I'd come home. They've arranged for a therapist to come to my house daily but I still kind of feel numb. How about you?"

There was a long pause.

"It's bizarre being home, are you sleeping at all?"

"A few snatches here and there but not really and I keep waking up to being drowned again."

"Same here."

We both sighed.

"It's so lovely to hear your voice again."

We caught up.

"Well love, I have a question for you. Would you be willing to come to Chicago to be on Oprah with me and tell the story of what happened?"

I froze.

"We could get to see each other again. Oprah's people contacted me and said they'd love to tell my story on the show. It's going to be a Tsunami Special, and they would be able to raise a lot of money through Oprah's Angel Network from the program, which we could donate to Pottuvil and Arugam Bay. I think we could raise a lot for the area. There won't be any administrative fees on the money as it will go directly there, and given Oprah's profile it could be a large amount. It's not like a regular NGO where there will be lots of expenses, and who knew we would get the opportunity to see each other again so soon? I'd love for you to come if you feel up to it. It's all expenses paid, they will arrange the flights and a hotel for you to stay in and you won't have to lift a finger, and you can even bring someone with you if you want someone to support you. We're also inviting Sri, the Swedes and The Squires too, so we'll all be together again. What do you say?"

"Yes!" I replied immediately without pause. I was desperate to be reunited with Nate and the others and it would be amazing to be a part of something that was raising money for charity for the area I had survived from. I'd get to see Nate, and Sri hopefully too, plus Annelli and Stefhan.

"You can take a little time to think it over if you like but that's awesome! I can't believe we're going to see each other again so soon. But take the day to think about it, speak to your mum and see what she says. Oprah's people will be in touch with flights and hotel bookings and all the other logistical arrangements. I can't wait to see you!"

"Me too, Nate, me too." And for the first time that week a hint of a smile crossed my face.

I told my mum who was with me immediately.

"That was Nate on the phone Mum. They are doing an Oprah show on the tsunami and on Nate's story and he's invited me to go on the show with him."

"Wow, they invited you to go on Oprah. That's great, will you go?"

"Yes, I think so, what do you think? It's going to be to raise money for Arugam Bay, so I really want to be a part of that to be able to give back. I can take someone with me too if you want to come?"

"If you're going to go to Chicago to do the show and feel well enough, I will go back to Pakistan to continue with the shopping for Anita's wedding. Or do you want me to come with you to Chicago?"

"No, I can go alone."

And just like that I was going to Chicago.

I needed to get a new passport. So far, I'd only left the house on Jo's insistence to get check-ups and see doctors. I secretly wondered if I had the mental strength to deal with the outside world when I was still so fragile but the pull to be back with our gang and be reunited with Nate was stronger.

Work had seen the news, and given I was a contractor and not due to be back till the end of January, I had let them know I was alive and needed to probably take an extended break before I would be able to return. They were understandably very accommodating and wished me well and were relieved to hear that I had survived.

One of the nicest things I remember was one day I popped into my local deli to get some cheese and bread and the owner, a tall, big burly man called Chris, came straight from behind the counter and gave me a huge hug. "I didn't know if you were alive or dead." He exclaimed, surprised I looked at him, touched by his kindness and genuine outpouring of warmth. We had shared the odd glass of wine with each other on my way home from work when I would pop in to get my dinner for the night and would chat here and there. My eyes pricked with tears, even though I had felt I wasn't worth saving, others, even people on the periphery of my life were happy to see me alive and would have missed me if I hadn't survived.

I called Sri to see if she too was going but she had declined as they were now in Australia and Wayne was still in the hospital. I was disappointed that they weren't coming but understood. Wayne's infection had gotten worse, and he was on IV antibiotics for months after the tsunami.

Nate was true to his word and arrangements were made and before I knew it, I was in Chicago!

I had an extra day before the show and Nate had invited me to his home for dinner. A car was sent to pick me up and as I stood outside his door waiting for him to answer the bell, I wondered what it would be like to be reunited again.

It was warm in his corridor while I waited bathed in a warm light as I stood there nervously.

The door opened and there was Nate, and we were instantly in each other's arms embracing. A warm feeling deep inside my belly rose as my heart filled simultaneously. To know that you weren't mad and to be with someone else that had experienced the same, no worse, horror than you had, the trauma bond you shared that no one else could really comprehend.

I felt safe there with him at that moment. He led me into his palatial apartment, beautiful and sophisticated just as I would have expected from a highly successful interior designer. It was beautiful, classic and minimalist. His home felt warm, inviting and refined.

Nate had ordered some food, and as he unpacked it we sat at the table with a glass of wine and discussed how it had been for us both coming back and relaxed in the familiarity of our shared experience.

"How have you been adjusting, Ani?"

"Badly. In fact, very badly. You? Are you getting any sleep? I can't get any before dreaming of drowning again."

"Same here. I am in a nightmare. My parents have sent me a therapist who comes to see me daily, but it sounds so weird when talking to them about it."

"It feels like we must have made it up; it's such a horrific and bizarre story."

Dinner was a comfortable and cosy affair, just us, allowing us to speak openly and freely about life in the aftermath. We shared stories of sleepless nights, therapists, and doctor's appointments. How everything felt so incredibly bizarre once your world had been turned upside down by being in a tsunami and the difficulty, we both had to adjust to 'normal' life once we got back.

Nate had also experienced the same discombobulation that I had upon arriving back to his apartment.

Why was everything still in its place? Shouldn't it have all been upside down and smashed to smithereens? We laughed conspiratorially at these idiosyncrasies that we had developed and how those around us thought we were probably nuts.

I finally broached it.

"Still no sign of Fernando?"

"No. They searched the area for days after, but they couldn't find him. The show will also be a tribute to him."

The next day we were due to record and a car came to pick me up and took me out to the studio.

I was led down the stairs to one of the green rooms. The hairstylists straightened my hair and the make-up girls applied foundation, to cover up my scars, and blush to bring some colour into my cheeks.

My heart was in my mouth, the girls around were fussing a bit of eye shadow here, and some lip liner there while they made me look presentable. Friends had commented quietly when they thought I wasn't listening to how my face looked frozen when I got back. Paralysed by fear, like a rabbit in the headlights, did I look like that now I wondered? Well, I was here now, and the show was being done one way or the other.

I was prepped, preened, hair straightened, and my highlights caught the light with streaks of copper, and blonde.

Well at least I looked OK I nervously thought.

A producer came in.

"Hey Ani, I'm just going to take you through what's happening on the show and when you'll be called up. Is that OK?"

"Sure," I croaked.

Nate left me in the green room to start the show while I waited with the other guests. Anneli and Stefhan were there, along with the Squire family. We all embraced in a huge hug delighted to see each other again so soon after the tsunami. We learnt we had all been struggling with the same things which merely made us feel even closer than before. Anneli and Stefhan caught me up on their stay in hospital where they had been taken care of for a few days after. The Swedish health care system put ours to shame, they had doctors, psychiatrists all on hand 24/7 to help them recover. Quite a lot of Swedes were lost in the tsunami, one of the highest casualties in Europe, just over 500 people and the nation was mourning the loss of so many of their young people.

The entire Squire family – Phillip, Louise and kids Emma, Laura and Will had also made the trip out and I embraced them as we talked about leaving cold England to come to an even colder Chicago with the wind whistling through the streets. I exchanged numbers with the Squires' and we promised to stay in touch when we got back to the UK.

Most of our injuries were getting better, no longer visible as our limbs were covered up. Louise told us of her extensive medical treatment she needed after her bite with the snakes and being attacked by ants. The kids looked remarkably resilient given what we had faced. Everyone was happy to be alive and reunited once more. All of us were the 'walking wounded.'

The producer put mics on us and led us to the audience where we were seated. I noticed the pictures of Oprah with her famous guests over the years adorning the studio walls as we were led down the dimly lit corridor.

We were to watch the show from the front row and when it was our turn to go on stage for our segment.

A frisson of excitement was coursing through me along with the nervousness, the audience were warm and empathetic. Coming from the UK we were not used to the level of adoration of celebrities here. Clearly, they loved Nate and were moved by his story, crying and dabbing at tears as they showed the introductory footage.

Nate told the whole story of his holiday with Fernando and then the terrible day. He spoke of the search efforts but he had never been found.

A beautiful tribute to Fernando played out on the studio screens as they collected various footage of him, and his life, pictures of him alone and with Nate as well as his famous photography showing stills of some of his more iconic images. Fernando's family were also sitting in the audience on our row, and they cut to his brother for a brief interview.

I felt big tears slide down my face. It was funny as I found myself holding my breath while watching the footage suspended in shock and horror all at the same time. The more times you'd watch footage, the more you'd wonder how on earth you managed to survive; it just didn't make any sense.

After they did the introduction and tribute to Fernando, they moved the focus to Nate's story and how he survived. They started with Nate when he first met Anneli just after one of the waves had begun to subside. She had told him to run for higher ground because another wave was coming.

I hadn't heard this all before and listened intently drawn into the horror of the story.

"How did she know such a thing?" Oprah asked. She turned to Anneli.

"I worked as a journalist a couple of years ago and I did a feature story on tsunamis in Hawaii," Anneli said. "I spoke with some professionals in Hawaii about how a tsunami works in the minutes between the waves, and what you should do during a tsunami. After the first wave, when we went through the laundry, I walked down to the Galaxy Hotel, and I saw that all the buildings were gone. And I also walked down to the beach because I wanted to see if it was only a really high tidal wave or if it was a tsunami. When I saw the ocean floor, and that the whole ocean was gone, I knew that this was a tsunami. This is really big. Run for your life!" Anneli relayed.

Gasps in the audience went around as they heard this and imagined the horror.

The Squire family were up next.

They were in the hotel restaurant when the tsunami hit.

"I opened the door [to the restaurant bathroom] and that's when the first surge of water came into the bathroom and just raised very quickly until I was flat against the ceiling," Emma said.

"As soon as I got out of the bathroom, I was slammed into a palm tree. I felt myself losing consciousness and the blackness covering my eyes. I was positive I was going to die. There were bodies floating with me that would bang into my body."

Each member of the family struggled to survive, while fearing the others were dead. Phillip even witnessed a building collapse on his wife, Louise. "I thought there's no way that my wife would be able to survive the strength of that wave," he said. "I decided that I would go into the waves and see if I could find her. I felt that if she had got a concussion of some sort, that I would be able to find her and save her."

Phillip started searching. He stumbled upon Emma, dazed but alive. They waded through heavy currents of water back to reach their hotel. Amazingly, they discovered Laura and Will there. They were back at the hotel just minutes before the second wave hit.

When they reached higher ground, they came across Nate who had been in the same hotel as them. He said that he thought he had seen Louise and she was alive.

It was my turn to take my seat on the mustard-coloured leather sofa that everyone was sitting on.

As they went to a break people shuffled around to make way for me to sit next to Nate who was sat next to Oprah, and they all sat to the right of me.

Nate and I held each other's hands tightly for every second I was on stage with him, the warmth of his hand a reassuring presence helping me to get through my rattled worries.

Before they came to me, Nate and Oprah introduced me.

"Ani Naqvi was vacationing in Arugam Bay, Sri Lanka, when the tsunami hit. She is the first person Nate met when he made it to safety at the top of a nearby hill."

"In that situation where everything and anything's unfamiliar and Ani and I started talking, I learned that she had been a producer for the BBC. And if there's one thing that makes me feel comfortable, it's a producer. And I thought, 'OK, this is somebody who's going to be organised, have it together, be able to coordinate everything that needs to be coordinated,' and we just looked at each other and I think at that moment, there was just kind of a trust there between us."

"Nate's instinct was correct! Ani commandeered the cell phone and got on the phone with the British Foreign Office and the BBC, she called the world desk."

Ani was our first and constant and accurate source of information," Nate explained. "Because we didn't know what had happened."

Taken from (Source Oprah.com)

"Ani, you've been through a tsunami, you've seen death first hand, experienced near death and wasn't it you that a palmist had predicted that you would have a near death experience?"

"Yeah" I nodded my head in acquiescence.

"Yeah tell me about that," Oprah asked softly.

"When I was trapped underneath the building and it was the second time I thought I was going to die and I was drowning, I'd had my palm read a few years ago and what they said came to me at that point, they predicted that I was going to have a near death experience but I was going to survive it and at that very moment while I was trapped underneath this building the force of the wave managed to shake the building away and I managed to get free from it and managed to come up for a gasp of air at that very same time." I replied nervously, my words all jumbled up, (even constructing a simple sentence was challenging for me at that time).

"Wow, when you were thinking that thought?" Oprah asked.

"Yeah." I nodded again.

"And how did you get to the hilltop?" she continued.

"After the first wave I met up with my friends Sri and Wayne who I'd seen as I was being tossed around in the tsunami and managed to hobble over to them cos I had got a few injuries on my legs and we were wondering around and eventually we heard the second wave coming and we ran up inwards / inland and a local person told us "to come this way" and took us to safety and then we kind of walked up to the hill from there." I replied.

"And tell me, I love this story of how you first met Nate." Oprah smilingly asked me.

I laughed as I looked up at Nate who was also smiling warmly with our recollection of that first moment we officially met as our faces lit up recalling the scene.

"We were congregating around the jeep that had the telephone and they were slicing up some pineapple and I had a slice of pineapple in my hand and Nate asked me if he could have some of my pineapple." I looked over at Nate smiling with him also laughing and continued on, "And I sort of hesitated for a moment, because the pineapple was actually for my friend Sri who was pregnant at the time and so I kind of looked at it and looked at him and thought yeah of course and waited for the next slice of pineapple to take over to her."

"What do you struggle with now that you are home?" she continued.

Tears pricked my eyes and my face scrunched up as I recalled the more painful aspects of the aftermath. My big, dark brown eyes filled with water and reddened as I answered.

"It's very difficult to get your life back together again after going through something like this," I replied.

"But the support of friends and family is really helping. But you are changed. You've been through this horrendous experience and seen so much death and destruction around and devastation and the people there have lost so much and the people that have lost people like Nate and Richard....It's so sad, but you have to take some solace in the fact that you/we were saved.

"I think that we owe it to ourselves and to the people that lost their lives to make the most of our lives and what we have left.

"I know I must have been saved for a purpose; I believe the soul leaves earth when it has gotten whatever it has come for. I don't know what that purpose is now. But I'm sure that it will become clear as time goes on. But I do think there was a purpose in us being saved because it was a miracle that anybody survived. It really was."

Taken from (Source Oprah.com)

Little did I know that these sentences I spoke to Oprah in mid-January 2005 just weeks after the tsunami laced with a huge amount of survivor guilt and an awareness that comes from having survived near death would set me on a path to my purpose and be the catalyst for a seismic transformation in my life.

The next day I was back in London to pick up the rest of the pieces of my life.

TWENTY-NINE

A Downward Spiral

The next three months back in London were some of the toughest of my life. I took a leave of absence from my job and mostly stayed at home. I slid into a deep, dark, depression.

Sri was on the other side of the world in Australia with my other bestie Xan who happened to be there on a six-month trip, but the distance felt more than miles.

Wayne was still in hospital in Australia and quite critical at the time. We found out Sri had broken a couple of ribs, which would have accounted for her quiet pained looks in the aftermath. The baby luckily was doing OK and had suffered no damage which was a huge relief. But understandably Sri was preoccupied with the father of her baby making it and trying to overcome her own trauma of having lost her home and hotel she had so painstakingly and lovingly built for the past few years.

Now there was nothing left of Galaxy hotel but the local people she employed who were like family to her needed more than ever work and support in the aftermath of this catastrophic disaster. Her own version of PTSD had her trying to rebuild what she had lost as quickly as possible with the backdrop of all that going on.

I was dealing with my own demons. My inner critic had a field day and Sri being so far away and caught in her own world brought them out even more.

"See no one loves you," it would hiss. "Sri has left you; no one will ever love you, not even your best friend. She doesn't think of you as her sister, only you. You're going to die alone. You're unlovable, ugly and mean."

On and on the inner demon would relentlessly spin its web of lies hatching one negative spiral after another. Confirming all those dark thoughts that flew around in the safety of the inky veil it created.

I was finally diagnosed with posttraumatic stress disorder and saw a trauma psychotherapist for treatment, the same doctor who counselled people captive in Guantanamo Bay and was a renowned natural disaster therapist.

He used Eye Movement Desensitisation and Reprocessing (EMDR) therapy which focuses directly on a memory and is intended to change the way that the memory is stored in the brain, to help take away the emotional charge from some of my more horrifying nightmares.

A couple of months later I'd attempted to go back to work, but things were different. I was changed forever and found it difficult to navigate normal life after the extreme of what I'd been through.

I requested a desk change so I was looking out at the office rather than facing the wall so I could spy a wave crashing through the windows in case there was ever such a thing in central London. I realise these were irrational fears, but I had never imagined being in a tsunami despite my many death fantasies.

Everyone was sympathetic and asked a ton of questions, but every time I'd tell the story it was like reliving the whole thing over and over.

"How did you get out?

Could you swim?

How did you escape the second wave?

Were you in it?

How were you saved?"

They would probe. Gasps and looks of horror would descend on their faces but it was as though I was telling a story that wasn't quite real. No one could really understand the impact even after I regaled all the intimate and fantastical data, it was just another story like a newspaper that they could move on from and forget but there was no respite for me.

I couldn't participate in normal activities anymore. I couldn't do small talk by the water cooler. I didn't want to go to drinks after work and socialise anymore. I didn't care about presenting what seemed like pointless presentations.

I felt lost at sea literally and figuratively. I was there but it felt like I'd disappeared. My soul had jumped ship waiting out in the wings unsure of whether it would be safe to come back; I'd even managed to scare my very being away.

I was a shell of a person. Of whom I had been. A physical presence but that was all.

The world and my work seemed so pointless considering what I had seen and been through. Who cared about creating spreadsheets and PowerPoint presentations about revenue, project progress and delivery?

It was all so meaningless in the grand scheme of things.

I found it impossible to go back to that life while I grappled with a very real existential crisis.

I left work for good shortly after as it all felt so pointless and retreated home.

Why me? I kept asking myself.

How did you do it? Others would often ask.

Did I fight for my life? Was I a strong swimmer? How did I make it and so many others died?

For some reason I had survived, whether it was to do with how I fought or the presence of a guardian angel saving me from death. On a later palm reading years after the tsunami a palmist told me a line on my palm indicated a protective shield or presence of a guardian angel saving me from death. So, who knows if it was all circumstance and luck as to whether I survived or not, or something else. The wave was so devastating and powerful that there was no control. I was completely and utterly powerless making it seem like I could swim out of it or that had anything to do with surviving isn't accurate as the force of the wave was so strong. Somehow, I made it out, and I just wasn't sure why yet.

THIRTY

Bell's Palsy Strikes

One cold, drizzly morning in March, just three months after I got home, I woke up and noticed drool down the side of my mouth and numbness on the left side of my face.

One side of my mouth and face wasn't moving. When I tried to speak I couldn't and when I took a sip of water (I'd stopped drinking JD and cokes for breakfast) in the morning it had missed my mouth and dribbled down my nightie instead.

It was not dissimilar to when you have a dental anaesthetic.

What the hell was going on now I wondered? As I looked at myself in the mirror, I noticed that the whole of the left side of my face was drooping, my eye was barely opening.

I panicked; I'd never experienced anything like this before. Did I have a dental problem? Or was it a stroke? It looked like the kind of face people have after having a stroke. I called out to my flatmate in a weird voice, as I couldn't speak.

"Jo! What's happened to me? My face is not moving," I muffled to her; my voice was so odd it was freaking me out.

She examined me.

"We need to get you to the doctor. Get dressed, I'll take you to the GP and they can take a look." she replied. I loved her no nonsense, matter of fact jolly hockey sticks kind of energy.

I did as she said as panic overtook me and I wondered when this hell would ever end, I thought hopelessly.

I was lucky and the GP was able to see me as an emergency case, but they were also not sure of what it was and sent me to the maxillofacial unit at St Georges Hospital to see a specialist.

I was finally seen by a specialist who ran a number of tests and eventually diagnosed me with a condition called Bell's Palsy.

Bell's Palsy is a condition where half the face becomes paralysed due to some nerve issue which can be caused by a few different factors, but one is a viral attack. They explained that given the extreme trauma I'd been through and subsequent infections and health issues my immune system was compromised, and a virus most probably had managed to attack the nerve causing the condition.

I stared at him processing this new set of terrors that had now befallen me. Would this nightmare never end? What more would I need to endure? Hadn't I suffered enough? I panicked.

"When will it get better?" I asked.

"Well, it's usually temporary, but it can last from three months up to a couple of years in some cases," he replied.

"But my sister's getting married in July. Will it be gone by then? I can't go to her wedding looking like Quasimodo!" More panic as my breath quickened as I contemplated being seen out in public looking like this.

Our Asian community could be judgemental at the best of times, with one aunty or another always commenting on how you looked. "Oh itney mote kasai ho gain?" Oh, how did you get so fat? Or "itney kali quo hogain?" How did you get so dark?"

My mum already had enough to contend with me as the 'black sheep' in the family. Unmarried at 33, single and living on my own in London while my sister who was ten years younger was already getting hitched. If this wasn't scandal enough now, I would not only be the freak show person who survived the tsunami and all the tsks of judgement as to why these disasters came crashing through my door but now there would be an even further ignominy of me looking like I'd had a stroke.

Imagine if this had been in 2024 in the age of Instagram my life could have been over publicly.

It's a pretty common understanding that in the Indian sub continental culture beauty, fairness, attractiveness as well as education, status and job position and income were all revered. In the same way my parents had been against me becoming a journalist, it was suddenly OK once I became a journalist for the BBC because that had more status and respect internationally. People loved the BBC from that part of the world.

Well, they would have a field day with me, looking like this, whispering behind my back, sniggering and gossiping. That is what I told myself. It was an indication of my own putative thinking.

"Hmmm, well, the wedding is not that far away so I can't guarantee that it will be gone by then." He replied and there I was in the pits of despair again.

I got back into my flat and sat down hard. I picked up my phone and called my mom.

"Mum, I've got something wrong with me, some paralysis on the side of my face. It's called Bell's Palsy." I slurred to her, my voice sounded like I was drugged and came out in a series of grunts and noises rather than fully formed words. Spittle dribbled down the side of my mouth, which I apparently had no control over. Another thing I had no control over.

"What, what do you mean? What's wrong with your voice?" She replied, unable to understand what the hell I was trying to say.

"It's this thing I told you about the Bell's Palsy. It's affected my face and my speech, look. But don't worry I will be fine." I switched on the video so she could see me.

"Anila what's that?" she shrieked. I feel sorry for my mum, she had such a difficult life, first my dad and me, her eldest, suffering so much. But that was life, no one was immune to pain and suffering indeed they lived side by side of pleasure and acceptance.

"I'll come on the next flight," she announced.

"Don't worry Mum, it will be OK." I said but secretly I was relieved she was coming. I was an independent person having lived on my own since the age of nineteen but right now I felt like I was drowning again, and I needed her.

Mum arrived the next day and the next few weeks I barely left the house.

On top of the PTSD, I became self-conscious about the way I looked; it seemed my nervous system was mirroring my inner turmoil into a very real paralysis on my physical body. But directly on to my person and face almost like I couldn't hide the trauma from myself let alone from other people.

While inside all I wanted to do was hide, curl up into a ball and disappear, forget it ever happened, ignore it but the drooping on my face was a constant reminder of my inner shutting down, my nervous system stretched to breaking point.

I cried myself to sleep every night fretting and did a ton of research where I found out that acupuncture treatment on the face with electrical stimulation could speed up the healing process.

Luckily there was a holistic therapy room just across the road from my house, literally a stone's throw away where there was an acupuncturist, and I went to see him for a consultation.

"Yes, I can help with this." He reassured me. He went on to explain how it was a stagnation of Qi and was called Zhong Feng in Chinese Medicine. Which translated means Wind Attack. Wind or air is thought to enter the body and attack the vessels in the face he explained to me. This can then result in Qi (energy) and blood stagnation stopping the channels from nourishing the affected areas on the face.

I thought it ironic that I was named after the Air / Wind Gods in Hindu mythology and here I was being attacked by 'wind" in Chinese medicine.

"How quickly can you get rid of it?" I asked desperately.

"If we do treatment regularly, I can use electrical stimulation too and it can help reduce symptoms quickly."

"I can come daily if necessary." I replied.

"Even better."

I went to see him as often as I could, and he placed needles in my face and attached electrical nodes to the needles sending small electrical currents to stimulate healing. It was a strange feeling having your face mini electrocuted but fear of looking like this permanently spurred me on.

I was lucky and the acupuncture did indeed speed up my healing and within a month I was much better, but my eye still drooped and to this day still has a vestige of that drooping.

Mum looked after me, she cooked and cleaned and fussed over me. She cooked my favourite dishes at first even if eating them was no mean feat when you could only move half your face, so she switched to liquid food when she saw how I struggled with the simplest of basic tasks such as eating.

Her heart broke time and time again as she saw me suffer and she was torn between wanting to stay with me but also not being able to get much time off work. A few days later she turned around to me and spoke.

"Why don't you come and live in America with me and your sister? I can take care of you properly there; you don't have to stay here on your own."

"I'm not on my own though, I have Jo." I replied.

"Yes, but I want to look after you and I can't take time off indefinitely otherwise I'll lose my job. And you need your family at a time like this, Jo has been great, but you need family, I can take care of you there and your sister is getting married soon too."

I considered her offer, I kind of wanted to stay home but I was still not well.

"You can come and help us with Anita's wedding preparations too. You must come there anyway, so you will just come a little earlier," she offered as a little something knowing that I wanted to be involved with the planning. Despite having PTSD I was still very protective and felt a responsibility towards my younger sister.

My sister Anita was ten years my junior and we were as different as chalk and cheese. She was the opposite of me in so many ways, having taken after my mum more rather than my dad. She was quiet and timid and kind and sweet and had fallen in love with her betrothed a few years ago but he'd only just come round to falling in love with her.

It was the biggest event in our family for years until the tsunami had gotten in the way.

Mum continued pleading with me over the next few days till I finally capitulated to her request, and we decided to put the house up for rent while I would go back to the USA with her to convalesce.

Shortly after I flew out to America and another chapter in my life started.

While I was in America, mum and the rest of the family coddled me, and I began to recover slowly but surely.

My sister's wedding was a huge source of happiness and a massive distraction from my trauma and the tsunami. I'd always fancied myself, as a bit of a wedding planner it seemed like a good use of my project management skills and my sister was a very detail-oriented bride. Bridezilla is the word that came to mind!

She wanted everything to be just right and chose her colour scheme in line with her clothes, flowers to match, expensive and grand hotel room booked, and catering ordered.

She obsessed over each (what seemed to me minor) detail, the centre pieces needed to match this or that and the wedding would be one of the largest the Naqvi clan had ever seen, busting in at over four hundred people. I organised her Mayun and Mehndi ceremonies, sorting out decorators, buying crepe paper, party plates and cutlery etc, ordering some of the younger cousins around to do this or that, to place the banner a little higher, a little lower, no left, now right and so on.

I chose the menu with her approval and negotiated a great deal with the best Pakistani caterers in the area who had given me an extra discount on account of the fact we were both from London.

In those months of May and June my nightmares had lessened.

I would often sleep through two or three nights at a time without having one. I was able to drive a car again and I was able to talk normally to others and my Bells Palsy was clearing.

Dad was coming over for my sister's wedding too, which was scheduled for mid-July. It would be the first time I'd seen him since the tsunami and the first time I would have seen him in five years.

My relationship with my dad was complex understandably given our difficult history. On the one hand I was more like him than I was like my mum.

I too had an avid interest in politics. He had dabbled in Pakistani politics in his day. We both had vices like drinking and smoking. I had his gregarious nature and intellect and when he wasn't angry, he was fun, engaging and entertaining. He attracted friends to him and I'm sure was an interesting and popular man in his social circle. But to me, like many of our parents, he had long been a difficult man.

When he arrived in Houston he was gruffly happy to see me. We'd had to prise him away from his work as a Barrister in Pakistan for the wedding. He was finally enjoying some success in his career, which had eluded him when we lived in London. Back then in the 70's there was still so much racism for an immigrant like him and he'd struggled to make his law practice a success in London, finding that the old boy's network was a clique cut off from him with his immigrant status.

My whole family was together. Slowly the pieces of my life began to come together.

PART II
Picking Up The Pieces

THIRTY-ONE

Drawn to Danger

Finally, I was coming back to London to get a permanent job and had an interview in just a couple of days.

Summer in London was glorious, even if the city were on edge from the recent July 7 terror attacks. This was a series of suicide bombings that had been a co-ordinated attack on my city. The bombs had gone off on Tubes and Tube stations killing 52 and injuring hundreds others. I'd gone to visit Nate during the summer that year while in Houston and he was driving me to the airport when the news came on about the attacks. We spoke about it, and I admitted how relieved I was that I hadn't been in London at the time. I think it would have been too much trauma in a short space of time to manage with and it was also strange I happened to be with Nate at the time we heard about it. Serendipitous.

At the end of the summer I'd gone back to London life and settled back into a familiar routine. I was commuting to work, expending energy on expanding my department's function and recruiting young talented staff to help me spearhead the growth of the business.

I was part of the senior management team and people listened to me. As a contractor you didn't get this involved in organisational development but when you were permanent you had the ability to shape the landscape.

My job gave me focus for a while, but I slipped back into old habits of working too hard, playing too hard and self-medicating to numb the pain.

In those days PTSD and the effects of it were not as widely spoken about as they are today. In my quest to appear strong, and capable I had denied myself the compassion I needed to overcome this cataclysmic event and soldiered on.

I had treated the physical symptoms, but the psychological ones were just starting to show.

I was forever feeling guilty that I had 'made it'.

I heaped pressure on myself to 'make something of the second chance I had been given'.

I had thought that I'd feel galvanised after the tsunami and 'snap' out of my depression but much to my chagrin this wasn't the case. The cloud of darkness covered me like a veil once more as we headed into winter months and the hope I'd felt in the initial aftermath faded back to the dullness and darkness once more.

The tsunami was a metaphor for my life, with huge waves crashing into me, holding me under while I struggled to stay afloat and get the breath in that was vital to life itself. My life was the same, colossal traumatic events engulfed me and held me down as I struggled to stay up on the surface gasping for air, simultaneously going back under again for periods of time only to emerge for another snatch of air and repeat the same process. Only instead of being over minutes it was long and drawn out.

I used my job as a distraction rather than confronting my healing head on.

Three years dragged on.

The urgency around making my life more purposeful and meaningful started biting at my heels again.

The war in Iraq had been going on since 2003 and it had become clear that there were no weapons of mass destruction. I had been one of the millions that had marched against the war so when I found myself with the opportunity to work in Iraq for an international NGO in Baghdad I jumped at it. It was now 2008 and at the height of the war.

Before I knew it, I was having a farewell party to leave for Baghdad's Red Zone for an assignment as Head of Programs for the International Medical Corps. In Baghdad during the war there was a town within the city around ten square kilometres called the Green Zone. This is where most NGOs would base themselves. My NGO however wasn't in the Green Zone! Rather they felt they needed to be in 'real Baghdad' to deliver projects to those displaced by the war. We were in what was called the Red Zone in Baghdad which simply meant normal Baghdad without the protection of being in the enclave of the Green Zone!

My friends thought I was nuts.

For the first time since the tsunami, I finally felt like I was back on track with my intentions of contributing to society and fulfilling the purpose I was convinced I'd been saved for. I flew to Amman, in Jordan and then connected to Baghdad. There were no direct commercial flights at the time on account of the war and the plane from Amman was a tiny plane carrying army personnel, security advisors as well as NGO staff.

As we landed the plane circled in a corkscrew making me feel queasy and it juddered and shook, I gripped on to the arm rest as this felt super dangerous and I was already scared of arriving at a war zone. Not knowing what to expect, would there be firing in the streets? People running around shooting? I had no idea.

My driver-come-bodyguard had been one of Saddam's daughter's bodyguards (according to his own account) picked me up at the airport and we drove to the compound in the Red Zone.

The city was devastated, bombed out buildings, shells of empty, abandoned offices, crumbling walls and rubble on the side of the road from the deluge of bombs they'd endured. Huge office buildings lay empty with windows bombed out and half-built structures there. The destruction reminded me a little of post tsunami Sri Lanka. I scanned the outside as we drove around the city in our beaten-up car chosen specifically to blend into the surroundings. Kidnapping foreign NGO staff was big here so our security was of the utmost importance. My bodyguard had a gun in his back pocket reminding me of the danger we were in.

The compound where we were taken was a big house converted into an office space at the bottom and living apartments at the top.

The end of the road was barricaded with concrete bollards to prevent car bombers, and at the other end of the road were security guards with rifles.

This was to be our living and workspace the entire time. Due to security threats this meant we lived and worked in the same place without being able to leave so we never saw anything other than our four walls and occasionally myself and my colleague would have meetings at the Ministry of Migration who we were both supporting on different projects.

This was the toughest thing to deal with and due to the extreme circumstances, we worked for six weeks straight then had a week off where we could leave to go to Amman.

Effectively we were prisoners in the compound. We could not even stop and visit one of the street side restaurants or cafes.

With my colouring I could pass for an Iraqi, but I usually travelled with my colleague and he was Caucasian and blonde, so together we stuck out like a sore thumb.

There would be around ten bombs going off per day in the city, and our building would shake from the impact. I quickly got used to the sound of bombs and the building shaking.

One night I called my old friend Xan in Scotland.

"How's it going over there Ani?" Xan asked.

"It's hard living and working in the same space with the same people over and over," I replied.

As we were talking some gunfire went off outside, close enough to our compound for her to hear it.

"What's that noise?" she asked.

"Oh, that's just some shooting in the background. It happens all the time," I replied blasé.

There was a brief silence on the other end of the phone.

She sucked her breath in.

"Are you crazy Ani? What are you doing there? That sounds like it's right outside. Are you in danger?"

"Yes, it is close. But you get used to it after a while. It's normal here."

But that conversation made me realise the extremes of the decisions I made and that I was living in a proper war zone, just as I had always wished for as a teenager, when I wanted to be a journalist. I'd left one disaster zone, the tsunami, for another!

Did I now have a taste for this life, I wondered to myself.

That same night I got a real fright. The Country Director ran up the stairs with some other security personnel. He stuck his head into our apartment on the way up and told us to stay away from the windows as there was a mob with guns coming our way.

They headed up to the roof laden with Kalashnikovs in the event we were attacked but it ended up being a false alarm and the mob turned off before they got to our street. We all breathed a sigh of relief.

That was one of the hairiest and scariest experiences. Another one I was clocking up.

I was seeking them out without knowing. I didn't realise at the time the toll living in a war zone, being surrounded by bombings, shootings and living like a prisoner in the compound was having on me until I got back to London later that year.

All that gun fire, bombing and death had made me think I needed to live big right now, but I ignored the tell-tale signs that things were not well and I again spiraled into a deeper abyss on my return.

I felt like I was forever climbing a slippery mountain ledge and losing my footing and falling back down again before climbing back up a little and repeating the same over and over.

I had told Oprah I knew there had been a purpose in being saved but what that was still eluded me at this point.

THIRTY-TWO

Finding Love

Survivor Guilt. That was apparently the term for what had happened to so many of us.

Survivor guilt is apparently a particular guilt that can arise from surviving a life-threatening event when others have perished. My doctor had diagnosed me with PTSD years before and said that this was a common symptom.

My sense of survivor guilt was driving me to make the most out of my life – all the time. It also pushed me to do what I could for the 'greater good.'

Six years after that day in Arugam Bay, I was starting to realise that day had changed everything.

I continued with this line of work, becoming the Head of Projects for the largest UK charity. I even joked that it would be the death of me as it was such a stressful job.

I was still single, working relentlessly and chasing disaster after disaster. I was popping Xanax like Smarties at the time and self medicating/numbing.

It was 2009, the year the world's financial markets crashed triggering a world-wide recession. The bottom fell out of both the charity sector and contractor markets as companies cut spending on programmes to ride out the recession. Jobless, I decided to revisit Sri Lanka and spent some time managing Galaxy Hotel for the summer months in 2009. It allowed me to rekindle my closeness with Sri whilst managing Galaxy, with often daily phone calls to check on one thing or another.

Her tsunami baby was no longer a baby. Luke was nearing five years old in July. She and Wayne had got married when they had returned from Australia months after the tsunami.

Nate and I had seen each other in Sri Lanka by chance in 2006 but since then not much.

It was now, the summer of 2010 and six years on from the tsunami. I was 38, alone and at a loose end in the middle of August, I yearned to go on a summer holiday.

It was a notoriously busy month, so I didn't fancy my chances. I searched for yoga holidays; a yoga holiday was easy, with organised classes and a ready-made group of like-minded females to keep you company.

Surprisingly I came across a holiday advertising a fantastic last-minute deal.

A holiday leaving in 48 hours to the Greek island of Lefkada with a company called Healthy Options. The holiday included all flights, accommodation, yoga, Pilates and fitness classes. The only catch, I had to book and go immediately. This ticked every box. It was what I needed in my life right then.

It was my first time visiting a Greek island and I eagerly watched the scenery as we drove to Vasiliki, the town on the southernmost tip of Lefkada. The island was green and lush, with undulating hills and a twinkly sea inviting you in with its serene, blue waters. Lefkada was one of the Ionian islands and I noticed its landscape was greener and more verdant than other Greek islands I'd seen on posters and billboards.

We were led to our rooms for check in and I was introduced to a charming, simple ensuite room in one of the three hotels they used to host people. Later that evening there would be a welcome chat with all the Healthy Options staff and a run through of all the activities for the week.

I'd decided I was going to focus on getting fit for the week, I'd been neglecting my health for a while now and a week of doing lots of yoga and going on bike rides felt like a balm for my soul. I was determined to get as fit as possible in that week and looked forward to the classes the following morning.

That morning the instructor was a man, not a woman as I expected. He was a swarthy man, dark skinned and with a shaved head. Andrea's olive-skinned appearance was on account of his Italian heritage. He was from the south of Italy near Naples, he told us. His skin tone was about the same as mine, maybe a little lighter and he had a broad, open face, roundish in shape with huge brown eyes with long, thick lashes.

He looked like a laughing Buddha as he sat at the end of the class guiding us through meditation and his voice was like liquid velvet with his strong southern Italian accent, deep and soft. His voice was enough to calm the most agitated of souls and I relaxed to the rhythm of his voice.

The days passed in a gentle reverie, classes in the morning and afternoon leaving the middle and hottest part of the day for you to laze around by the pool and make friends with others in the resort.

I'd already made friends, an Irish girl called Jane who I'd hung out with on the first day. We now sunbathed together and went to the same classes together and we whiled the time away on the beautiful island, with frequent dips in the pool or sea to cool down.

The next evening, I went to Andrea's evening class called yoga nidra. It was a guided lying down relaxation and meditation. I was overdue for a relaxation meditation and in much need of some respite. Andrea's dulcet tones and calm, strong, grounded presence was the perfect antithesis to my nervousness, and I found myself relaxing deeper and deeper as the meditation went on.

Suddenly I heard noise around and realised the class was over. What sorcery was this I wondered? The insomniac had managed to fall asleep to Andrea's voice in broad daylight with people all around me and felt amazing upon waking. His gentle crooning had whisked me off to a place no one had managed to get me to in years. I looked at him in a different light.

I realised he was actually really good looking, not in a conventional way maybe but there was a quiet strength about him that was compelling. He was a man of few words preferring to observe our gaggle of giggling girls than join in.

He was after all the only man in the group, predictably the guests were all women and all the other yoga teachers also.

As Jane and I headed off to dinner together I confessed to her.

"Andrea's quite good looking don't you think?"

"D'ya think so? Ah yeah, the man's not bad, not my cup of tea like." She replied in her thick Irish accent.

"Do you fancy him?" She asked as she looked at me staring at him in the distance with a soft look on my face. "G'wan you fancy him, don't ya?"

"Maybe. He's got a lovely voice AND I fell asleep in the yoga nidra class. I never sleep, let alone in broad daylight!"

"Ah yeah, I can see you've got it bad for him." Her blue eyes twinkled back at me mischievously.

"He's probably got a girlfriend." I dismissed it suddenly, not wanting to get my hopes up. Love hadn't gone so well for me these past years.

"Well, there's only one way to find out." Jane smirked.

"Why what are you going to do Jane?" I asked warily.

"You leave it to me." She winked slyly.

"Don't do anything to embarrass me!" My voice rose in a panicked alarm.

"Don't ya worry about a thing, I'll handle it."

Jane was a fun, young 30-something Irish girl. I was having fun, and this was much better than what I'd originally planned, which was days of gruelling activity.

The following day we decided to ditch Andrea's yoga nidra class in favour of cycling to the other side of the village.

We ordered our drinks as we watched the sky darken in the evening. Suddenly Jane nudged me, "Look Ani, there's your man." And sure, enough Andrea was pushing his bike along the road while he walked slowly and methodically.

"Hey Andrea!" We both called out waving.

"Hello." He replied in his honeyed tones while I swooned again at the sound of his voice.

"Why don't you come and join us for a drink?" Jane asked. I gave her a sideways glance silently thanking her for intervening and inviting him to sit with us.

"Would you like a drink?" I offered.

"No, it's o-kaay,"he replied in his thick Italian accent.

Andrea joined us, and we started chatting, and before I knew it, we were in an animated, excited conversation with each other, talking about my dreams to build a yoga retreat which was shared by him and finding out about what he did and how long he'd been here.

Time melted away as dusk turned to darkness and mosquitos started nipping our ankles but even the mossies couldn't dampen my excitement at the palpable electricity, I could feel between us.

Jane barely got a word in as we were vibing off each other. Finally, he got up to leave.

"Why don't you join us for dinner." Jane ventured. Honestly, she was THE best wing woman one could have.

"No, now I have to go home, to put my bike away and relax, maybe another time."

"Where do you live?" I asked curiously.

"My house is just there," he pointed to the right of the bar to his home which was just 20 metres or so from where we had ended up.

"Oh, so you live up this end of the village then?"

"Yes, I am the only one. All the others live in the main part of town."

And with that he turned around and left.

"Check out the sparks on you two!" Jane turned to me when he'd gone out of earshot.

"You think so?" I replied nervously excited and unsure of my instincts.

"Are you kidding?! You two were getting on like a house on fire! We've been sitting here for a couple of hours getting bitten to shreds!"

"Yeah, we did get on, didn't we?" I ventured.

I'd been so unlucky in love for the past decade, so I had almost given up hope of meeting anyone I liked again. But I really did like this guy, there was something about him, a presence that was unlike anyone else I'd met. He was special, not like an ordinary man, something I couldn't quite put my finger on. I loved being around him, his energy had the ability to soothe, and calm even me.

The following evening, I was tired again. I was determined to have an early night. It was Friday already, and I was supposed to be leaving to go back home on Sunday, but I really didn't want to leave this beautiful island. I'd gone to speak to the lady that managed the bookings about staying on for an extra week. She'd said I could, I'd need to pay for another flight back, but it was all possible.

As I was coming back at dusk from a massage, I attempted to slide into my room without the Irish girls seeing me but luckily this didn't work. They greeted me from the alfresco restaurant and waved manically, grinning from side to side.

"Ani, over here!" Still only wrapped in a towel and my bathing suit I headed over.

They both knew about my teacher crush already.

Karen, one of the yoga teachers, had confirmed that Andrea was single.

I noticed that Andrea was sitting at the front of the open air, beach restaurant with a couple of friends of his, and he was playing the guitar while they were all singing along.

"Check out your man on the guitar there," they giggled at me.

"Come on, have a drink." Jane urged.

"No, I can't," I protested, "I'm so tired!"

"You have to, your man is out." Jane cajoled.

"Yeah, but he's with friends', I said wistfully, staring in his direction.

"What if we can get them to join us for dinner? Will you stay out then?" They eagerly enquired.

"I'll stay out." I replied hopefully. I had no game when it came to dating anymore. Knock after knock had left me wondering if I would ever meet the 'one', or even if the 'one' even existed. But this was low risk, they would be the wing women leaving me to hide under their cloak of conspiracy.

A few minutes later the girls brazenly called out to Andrea and his friends to join us to which they replied for us to join them as they were laden with guitars and instruments.

"Come on then Ani." They conspiratorially whispered to me with twinkles in their eyes. Well, I could hardly refuse now they had set things up so nicely! There were three guys and us three girls, so it was perfect symmetry and we headed over with me still in my towel from my massage!

We started chatting and singing along to their songs, with the assistance of song sheets and got more and more raucous the more comfortable we felt with them!

A while after Jane asked them, "Would you like to join us for dinner in town?"

I looked over at her blushing. How did she do it I thought? But I suppose it's much easier for someone else to invite your crush out than it is for you and she was doing all the heavy lifting and inside I beamed with hope while at the same time my heart felt like it was in a vice- like grip whilst doing somersaults at the same time.

Butterflies had taken over my insides in nervous anticipation as they do when you really like someone as I waited for his answer with bated breath.

"Sì okaaay." He replied in his stilted Italian accent, and I breathed a sigh of relief.

"I need to go shower and freshen up first," I said.

We all agreed to rendezvous in an hour and head down to the main town together. I'd suddenly perked up with the prospect of hanging out with Andrea more.

I put on a little make up, just some lip gloss. I'd caught the sun nicely that week and had turned a golden bronze so I didn't need much.

Ready, nerves merged with excitement, I headed out to meet the gang.

As we headed into town Andrea and I naturally paired off together on the walk, continuing where we'd left off the night before. Soon we were in one of the village bars and ordering drinks. Andrea and I sat next to each other, our knees touching, and little shocks of electricity would go through me from time to time.

It became apparent we had separated from the rest of the group and by the early hours of the morning when everyone else was dancing in the club we headed back to where we lived.

As we were walking down the dimly lit beach, we passed another club that seemed quite lively when Andrea turned to me and said, "Would you like another drink?"

"Sure, why not." I replied not wanting the evening to end.

Before I knew it, we were in another club, this one busier than the last and the music much easier to dance to.

It was too loud to talk much, and we found ourselves swaying together in unison until slowly Andrea made his move clearly signalling his interest in me should I still be unsure.

That night cemented our relationship together and when I awoke the following morning I was racked with fear.

It was Saturday morning, and I was still due to leave the following day.

"I really don't want to leave tomorrow."

"So don't go," Andrea replied matter of factly.

My heart did mini somersaults and shortly after breakfast, I confirmed arrangements to stay on another week.

I decided to move my flight to the following Sunday.

THIRTY-THREE

Celebration and Despair (Again)

A month later after a long Greek summer where I met Andrea in August 2010 I went back to London. My sister had given birth to twins and I was heading back to Houston for their first birthday celebration.

As the month had progressed with Andrea, I was much surer of us. I'd booked two more flights to leave that had been discarded and ended up staying much longer than I had anticipated. Maybe this was my reward for having got through it all and life would be plain sailing from now?

I was looking forward to going to Houston and revelling in letting my family know that I had met the man of my dreams. Like many Asian parents they wanted me married off and had been anxiously stressing about my singledom at the 'old' age of 38. Well now I finally had some good news to tell them.

As I arrived in Houston, I turned to Mum.

"Ammi I have something to tell you."

"What?"

"I met a guy in Greece!"

She looked at me. "Really?"

"He's Italian. But he's lived in India on and off for the past 10 years. He works as a Yoga Teacher at the place I went to on holiday, and he even speaks some Urdu/Hindi."

My mother was watching me, with smiling eyes.

"He's really caring and kind, a good man. He's good looking, and I'm so happy with him. He's such a wonderful man, I never met anyone like that before. I feel like he's my soulmate Mum."

My voice was animated and elevated as joy seeped through every little particle of my being and I basked in the glow of having some happy news for my mum.

"Allah ka shukar! That's very good, I'm very happy, now maybe one day you will get married." She exclaimed.

"Ammi! We just met."

"Yes, I know but if you like him as much as you're telling me, and he likes you then Insha'Allah you will also marry him."

"Hopefully." I added coyly and dreamt of weddings and kids in the not too distant future. I had a planned holiday in Morocco coming up with friends and I wanted to invite him.

When we chatted later, I decided to make my move.

"Have you ever been to Morocco?" I asked.

"No, but I've always wanted to go," he replied.

I went in for the kill.

"Well Xan who is one of my besties is going to Morocco with her and her family and they have invited us to go with them. Are you interested?

"Of course," he said.

Yes!

I would now be going on holiday as soon as I got back from the USA to Morocco with my two besties and Andrea.

I was so excited I could pop. My fortune was changing at last! I grinned manically with happiness; life was just perfect right now. I'd finally met my soulmate; my sister's premature twin baby boys were healthy and now I was going on holiday with some of my favourite people in the world.

I continued floating on clouds feeling invincible and in love. A strong feeling that my life was finally turning a corner for the better started to blossom. After all these years of darkness, heaviness, misery and depression weighing me down I was finally experiencing the other side of the coin.

Andrea had booked his flight to arrive in London a couple of days before.

Pop, pop, pop, pop, I was popping with excitement just like a sherbet dipper, fizzing away unable to contain my bubbliness and happiness.

THIRTY-FOUR

Death Catches Me Up

I went out to run some errands with mum and my sister. As we were driving I suddenly felt a sharp stabbing pain in my chest. It appeared near my heart and towards the left and I gasped out in pain while taking the intersection towards Katy, our final destination.

I gasped and bent over.

"What's wrong?" my mum asked.

"I have a pain in my chest." I replied. I paused.

The silence was deafening as neither my mum nor sister said anything.

"I will go to the doctor to check it out." I reassured them.

"Please go soon," my mum said.

Truth was, I had noticed some changes in my body these past few weeks. I needed to get that weird pain in my chest checked out. But I had dismissed it, come on, how serious could it be? I was only in my 30s, probably just heartburn.

But over that week in Houston the pain crept back at times, coming on with sudden ferocity intermittently that I decided I must go to see my doctor as soon as I got back home.

As soon as I got back to London, I headed to the doctors nonchalant.

"How long have you had this looking like this?"

"Three months now, I noticed it in August."

"And the pain?" she continued.

"I've noticed the pain intermittently for the past month really."

"OK, well, I think you should get this checked out as soon as possible. I'll make a referral to the breast unit at St George's Hospital for a consultation and some scans."

Her urgency suddenly alarmed me, and I ventured, "What do you think it is? You don't think it could be cancer, do you?" I asked cautiously.

"Without scans I can't say, but I do think you need to get it checked out quickly. I've made an urgent request for you to see the breast oncologist at St. George's."

Panic began to set in as the words 'oncologist 'and 'cancer' were bandied around and my heart began to thud, feeling like it would quite literally jump out of my chest and start running for the hills.

I was no longer floating on a cloud – rather I was falling back down to Earth at breakneck speed without a safety net. My head pounded and filled with cotton wool as inside a voice screamed no, no, no!

Not again. No, no, no! My mind refused to believe and once more I tried to calm myself with it's probably nothing, but I wasn't quite as convinced anymore.

Later that day while on the phone to Andrea I divulged the latest to him.

"You know I mentioned that thing I noticed on my breast?"

"Si."

"Well, I went to the doctors about it, and she wants me to get it checked out at the hospital."

"OK, that's good."

"Well, it might not be great news." I said carefully wondering what his reaction would be. We'd only been together for a matter of weeks, what would he think Would he stick around? Would he run a mile? I wouldn't blame him if he did to be honest, he didn't really owe me anything did he? As my mind wandered frantically around, I held my breath in anticipation of his reaction.

"Well, when you know what it is then you can think about it, but don't worry now, it could be nothing," he replied matter of factly, and I let out my breath in relief. He wasn't running for the hills - yet.

The day of my hospital appointment arrived, and I headed to St George's to see the breast oncologist. I nervously waited for my name to be called and was seen by an Asian male doctor. His details on the website said he was an oncoplastic breast surgeon which did nothing to aid my fears and worries that were now howling around like banshees in the wild wind.

Finally, I entered the room. Niceties dispensed with; the doctor asked me to undress for a physical exam. I undressed behind the curtain and sat back while he asked permission to enter.

"Can I come in?"

"Yes."

He entered the cubicle, "Please bring your arms over your head." He instructed. Then he tapped and prodded my breast, feeling around my armpit and towards the middle of the chest.

"What do you think it is?" I asked.

"Well, this presentation is indicative of breast cancer," he replied.

The surgeon continued to talk but my brain had switched off and I tried to listen to everything he was saying but could only catch snatches of it. Time warped, first it speeded up to breakneck levels then it slowed down intermittently still I only caught snatches of what he said.

"Yes," I replied numbly.

He handed me some pieces of paper, with referrals on them and the rest of the meeting was a blur as I gathered my things. My legs felt like lead weights as the shock permeated my body, numb I left that hospital and headed straight to another for the scans.

As the 7th dawned, we headed to the next doctor's office, I bit my nails and skin furiously drawing blood from the cuticles I'd bitten too much. Nerves had taken permanent residence in my body and my eyes darted around anxiously.

The not knowing was doing my head in more than anything, at least once you know you can plan but this waiting game was enough to make anyone have a nervous breakdown. Finally, the hour was upon us as we entered the room.

By now the fog parted and I was surprisingly lucid and clear when the doctor was talking.

"As I suspected, we have a hormone sensitive Grade 2, Stage 2 ductal carcinoma in situ and a tumour measuring around 2.5 cm in the lower left quadrant of the left breast."

I let out a deep breath as finally I knew. And for a few moments a sense of calm descended.

I was shocked. I was so young for my diagnosis. But simultaneously I wasn't shocked at all. I had been heading towards something ever since I had walked out of that wave. PTSD, trauma, depression, at various points in my life were not exactly an affirmative yes to life.

But in the eerie fearful state of my mind, a voice deep within spoke to me, the same voice that spoke to me in the tsunami:

"You will survive this, too. This will go on for 5 years, but you WILL survive." A calmness descended over me as I contemplated this deep knowing with my present day fearful, survival brain.

I left the hospital sometime later after the very kindly breast care nurses did what they did best. They comforted newly diagnosed patients with heart warming statistics and confirmation that they were making so many advances in drugs these days that survival rates were much better than they ever had been. Time after time the nurses impressed upon me that this wasn't a death sentence as everyone surely thought it was when getting diagnosed with the C disease. They tried to console and reassure me, but the tears that were welling up could be contained no more and big, fat, wet drops rolled down my face as I finally let go.

I only remember snatches of conversations and scenes, shock throwing a cloud of amnesia on me. I'm sure another way for the body to protect the mind from shutting down forever, permanently. How resilient we humans really are and how many ways we have of protecting ourselves from our biggest fear which will always be realised, the fear of death.

I went home dejected trying to process the information. At least Andrea was arriving later that day so I wouldn't be on my own at least.

The phone rang and I leapt to answer it. It was Andrea.

"I just arrived at Stansted airport. How did the hospital's appointment go?"

"Oh, I'll tell you when you get here." I replied dejectedly.

But he guessed from my reply that the news wasn't good.

The serendipity of Andrea arriving in London the same day of my diagnosis was not lost on me. Other than the friend who came to the hospital he was the only person who knew anything of what was going on. I'd not spoken to Xan, or Sri or anyone else about my appointments or examinations.

He arrived at mine, and I was uncharacteristically, eerily calm as I told him the news.

He put his arms around me while I sobbed on his shoulder. He was a man of few words but the words he did speak were profound and soothed away my fears.

"These things happen, everything will be OK," he quietly said with surety.

This sense of calm would come and go. In my wiser more mature moments, it would be a beacon of how I knew I could be. Until panic and fear would take over from time to and thoughts of death and mortality would dominate. This was normal I supposed.

With great challenge comes exponential opportunity and growth. However, sometimes when you're amid a challenge it's difficult to see the wood for the trees and it's only when it's behind us are we able to see the gift we were given in the new learnings we take away or new resilience we form.

I was forced to look at all aspects of my life in my analysis and examination of what had gone wrong and took me down this path.

But for now, I dealt with the immediate aftermath and wondered what to do about Morocco.

"What shall we do about Morocco?" I asked a bit later.

"What do you want to do?"

"I don't know, I think I want to go. I don't feel ready to decide about treatment options yet."

THIRTY-FIVE

Cancer Bites Hard

We arrived back from Morocco a week later. I was none the wiser about what treatments to do. I was still not ready to accept having a mastectomy, chemo, radiotherapy, which was what the doctor wanted.

Andrea and I headed to the planned hospital appointment together at St. George's. The doctor wanted to book the surgery.

"What if I don't want to do any of those things?"

"Well, then you'll need to see another consultant, an oncologist as I'm a surgeon so those are the options I can offer you. I can give you a referral. There's a doctor over at Marsden, he's the head of the Breast Unit there and is an oncology specialist so you'll be in good hands.

I breathed a sigh of relief as he filled out the paperwork and I felt like I had been given a stay of execution from chemo and surgery, a brief reprieve from having to deal with it all and the horrible treatments that were on offer.

On the way home Andrea turned to me.

"Ani, you have to tell your mum now, you can't put it off any longer."

I looked at him nervously, "Are you sure?"

"Yes, she needs to know."

"OK, I'll do it tomorrow." I replied dreading the moment I'd have to tell my mum.

When I told my mum, she got on the next available plane from Houston to London and arrived the following day.

A week later we told my dad of my diagnosis but swore him to secrecy as I wasn't ready for the entire Naqvi clan to know about my story.

So now I had Andrea living with me and my mum here to help. A few days later my mum urged Andrea to take me on a short break away from London to see if he could calm me down. So, we ended up in the New Forest but it was a wet and windy few days.

As we arrived back to London I didn't feel refreshed and recuperated just a heaviness descending over me.

We just walked back into my flat when my mum walked up to me, ashen faced. She looked at me hesitantly, quietly her lower lip quivering.

"Anila, I have some unexpected news from Pakistan."

"What?" I asked distractedly as I hung my wet clothes up.

"Your father passed away," My mum replied.

"What?" I replied in disbelief. My heart jumped into my throat as I choked out the words.

"Your father, he's dead. He died of a heart attack, Anila."

I stood stock still, not able to comprehend what she had just told me.

Slowly, her words sunk in.

"NO!" I screamed and suddenly all semblance of holding things together unravelled and I was falling again. The floor beneath me gave way and I collapsed in a heap on the floor as this new and shocking news so soon after my diagnosis seeped in.

"NO! NO! NO!" I wailed. The dam broke loose, and all the emotion and the tension of the past two weeks flooded out as I wailed on my living room floor while beating the floor as huge sobs and screams emanated from me. I sounded like a wild wounded animal being attacked by a lion with huge chunks being ripped from me and in excruciating pain.

In that second, I was taken back to Sri Lanka.

I was one of the Sri Lankan women lamenting the loss of their loved ones the day of the tsunami as grief and torment overtook me. Sobs racked my body as I wailed at the top of my voice uncaring as to who or what might hear me.

I thrashed on the floor at the injustice of it all.

"Why?! Why?! Why?! What did I do to deserve this? Why are you punishing me?" My eyes rolled upwards to an imaginary God.

A torrent of emotion rushed out.

Didn't I have enough to contend with? Was a cancer diagnosis not enough punishment that now my dad was also taken away? Before I could resolve my issues with him and find forgiveness.

"Do something; get her off the floor." My mother ordered, panicked.

Andrea didn't see anything wrong with my response though and quietly ignored her, leaving me to express my grief however I saw fit.

In those moments when I heard about my dad passing it was as if all the pain from the past was finally being allowed to pour out through grief.

The following days were some of the hardest. I was still coming to terms with my diagnosis.

The doctors had offered me the standard treatment of a mastectomy surgery, chemo, radiotherapy and hormone blocking medication. However, I wasn't ready for surgery and chemo scared me more than cancer itself. I knew they were telling me I had the Big C but I didn't feel ill. While I knew chemo would make me feel and look ill. It just didn't make any intuitive sense to me to destroy the entire immune system to kill cells that were dividing too fast.

I expressed my concerns to my oncologist and pleaded with him about other options. Luckily the Head of the Breast Unit at the UK's number one cancer hospital the Royal Marsden suggested I could start with hormone blocking medication in the form of a daily oestrogen blocking drug called Tamoxifen rather than full blown chemo and radiotherapy just yet. This sounded like a Godsend to me. It allowed me to buy some time before surgery and see if the Tamoxifen could shrink the tumour.

My mum asked the doctor, "What's the difference between her taking Tamoxifen and doing chemo?"

"There's not that much difference statistically with the outcomes only 1-2% difference but as Ani doesn't want to do chemo we need to take patient choices into account. This is a suitable alternative that has similar efficacy to chemo."

His reassurance had calmed her and she was on board with my treatment plan.

In the meantime I bought books on holistic and complementary treatments for cancer. I devoured Louise Hay's, *You Can Heal Your Life*, read David Hamilton's book, How your Mind can Heal your Body, "Dying to be Me" by Anita Moojani a lady who went into spontaneous remission after dying on the table, and would trawl cancer blogs for hours trying to absorb as much information as I could.

I had no control over anything, none of us really do but to someone who was a self-confessed control freak this wasn't acceptable. I tried to control what I could including my diet, taking supplements and starting a new fitness regime. Amongst countless other things.

I was plagued with a deep, chesty cough that I couldn't shake that took up home shortly after my diagnosis. Next I put my back out completely and was immobile and in excruciating pain due to sciatica. I felt at times that the whole world was against me. I lay awake at night hacking up pieces of my lungs as the winter nights drew in.

After a terrible Christmas in London long after my family had gone back home to Houston, Andrea whisked me off for a bit of winter sun to Sri Lanka.

Sri had invited us to stay at Galaxy Lounge. She was no longer there having moved to Australia, but we headed there anyway.

However, this wasn't like the time we'd been before during the tsunami or when I had been managing the Lounge briefly the year before. It rained every day and water leaked through the kadjun roof huts. My cough got worse and so we cut our trip short and escaped back to Colombo just days after arriving. Andrea was increasingly worried about my declining health.

In the dry, hot sunshine with 85% humidity my health began to slowly improve. We stayed in an apartment just off the sea and started the healing journey.

THIRTY-SIX

Remission? No Remission

For the next two years I threw everything at the cancer. I did daily yoga, meditated, studied Ayurveda and did acupuncture. I did foot detoxes, took supplements, ate 5-10 portions of veg a day, green juiced, drank distilled water, had my house energetically cleared and went on pilgrimages for healing. I tried a raw food health centre in Florida with Vitamin C infusions. Did an Ayurvedic detox called a panchakarma. Went to Peru to take plant medicines like Ayahuasca and San Pedro for physical and spiritual healing. I did liver detoxes, gave up drinking, partying, and adopted a healthier lifestyle in general. I visualised healing every day and reread books such as "Your Mind can Heal Your Body." I travelled to Italy to a cancer centre that used Hifu as an alternative treatment to chemo. It was only there that I found out I wasn't a candidate for the treatment. I tried flotation tanks, massage, and lymphatic drainage. I had spiritual healing, saw psychics and mediums, had more EMDR, and tried CBD oil.

You name it. If it could 'cure cancer' I would try it.

One of the many things I did was a yoga teacher training certification and yoga therapy course and that was where the door opened even wider to Ayurveda.

The more I learnt about Ayurveda the more fascinated I became and began to read extensively as well as signed up for a variety of courses both online and face to face.

I'd been following a doctor who was a prolific author on Ayurveda and was one of the key names on Ayurveda in the west.

He had his own centre in the USA where you could learn Ayurveda but he himself didn't see patients there. In fact, the only place he still saw patients was in his hometown of Pune where he had completed much of his training and had worked there for several years before migrating to the USA.

I pleaded with Andrea for us to go and try this treatment option. I was enamoured with Ayurveda already and I was drawn to seeing this particular doctor.

The first time I met Dr L he pressed down on a few marma points on my body gently with the gaggle of predominantly caucasian students watching eagerly. He had started by asking me my history of which I had told him the bare bones of what was going on and the medication I was already on.

As he pressed on the marma points he began to give me my whole history by asking a series of questions.

"Did you get a lot of bronchitis and tonsillitis as a child?"

"Yes."

This guy was clearly way more than just a doctor; he was deeply intuitive and highly knowledgeable about all aspects of Ayurveda. He could read palm, face and tongue, and was a master at pulse reading, all aspects of Ayurvedic healing that went so much deeper than the symptoms presented to Western doctors.

"Well, I will do my best to help you, but cancer is a tridoshic disease, and Ayurveda is best as a preventive rather than a curative. But we can have you take some scans now and try this for a period of three months and then do some other scans then to see if there has been any progress. If you can come here, I can also give you some marma point therapy."

I threw myself into the regime.

At the end of the three months, I went for another scan and eagerly brought my results to the clinic for him to study. I was convinced I was going to have good news. Nobody could do all these things.

"I'm sorry but there have been no significant changes in your scans."

My heart plummeted. I looked at him despondent and fraught.

"What should I do?" I asked him.

"I can't tell you what you should do."

"But if I were your daughter, what would you advise me to do?"

He paused.

"If you were my daughter, I would tell you to have surgery."

As the words came out of his mouth something inside me shifted. This was a man with a true gift who I respected as both an allopathic Western and Ayurvedic doctor and this was his advice.

It was now two and a half years on from my original cancer diagnosis. We were holidaying in the Andaman Islands for Christmas and New Year and it was eight years on from the tsunami.

It was a turning point.

A few days later I woke up on Christmas day in the Andaman islands and announced to Andrea.

"I think I need to have surgery."

"Really?" he enquired.

"Yes, it's time." So, we decided to cut our trip short to get ready to go home for surgery.

The Tamoxifen had indeed been working alongside other stuff I was doing. The cancer had shrunk in response to the treatments. Where there had been pockets of small cancerous cells all over now there was just one lump and smaller than before.

THIRTY-SEVEN

I opt for surgery

I was booked in the Spring 2013 to have a lumpectomy surgery; I had poured over dates depending on the waxing and waning moon as different times of the month had better and worse outcomes.

I stubbornly refused to have my lymph nodes out at the same time which just meant I would have another surgery to remove them six months later as scans over the summer would show them as growing, not subsiding as I had hoped.

The surgery was a day surgery and I reacted badly to the anaesthesia, feeling groggy and out of it for days. I was surprised by how difficult I found it to do small tasks like walk to the shops which were around fifty metres from my home. Once the effects of the anaesthesia wore off, I was stunned by how much more energy I had from before. Where I had always felt fatigued and exhausted now, I was full of beans and bouncing with energy. I suddenly realised how much having the cancer in me was draining.

Once I'd had both surgeries, I began to relax a little.

I was now officially cancer free finally for the first time in three years.

Andrea and I had been married a year. On our first trip together to the States, as expected in a family like mine, my mum decided to marry Andrea and I off. At first this caused many arguments but eventually mum got me to see her point of view and Andrea went along with it understanding the cultural differences. We were married in Houston in a traditional ceremony. I wore a wedding dress, a typical western ball gown, tight bodice and a billowing skirt with a wide net underneath. So far so western but the nod to my culture and heritage meant it was maroon in colour with delicate and tiny, hand applied gold embroidery in parts. Andrea wore a matching sherwani, a traditional dress for men with a hat/turban on his head and turned up uncomfortable shoes.

I was sure I was cancer-free and so I decided I didn't need the Tamoxifen anymore as I wanted to focus on getting pregnant now before it was too late. I had done so much to get my body back into homeostasis with everything I had done and was doing. I decided to do a panchakarma, which was an Ayurvedic detox while I was seeing Dr L on that course again. He was still treating me and was happy for me that I had done the surgery.

I worked hard all that year to stay clean.

I had my next check up in the spring exactly a year after my first surgery. I was shocked when the results came back with another tumour.

Every cancer patient's worst fear is a recurrence and now I had one. My world began caving in on me again as the illusion of any semblance of control over my world vanished once more. Panicked and with the same level of threat experienced by my first diagnosis I once again began spinning out. How was this possible I wondered to myself? Hadn't I changed everything? Done so much to alter my lifestyle?

Obviously stopping the Tamoxifen had been a bad idea and I berated myself as Pete Paranoia my negative inner critic had a field day with me.

"You stupid, idiot, look what you've done?" He screamed at me as fear had me in its grips.

Back in the hospital, the sound of the doctor's voice penetrated the fog while I attempted to take this new information in.

"You'll have to have radiotherapy this time, as you've had a recurrence within the year, we would seriously advise you to undergo this course of treatment in addition to recommencing the Tamoxifen. We'll have to get you booked in for another lumpectomy, luckily, we caught the lump early this time."

I would agonise over the decisions I'd made that got me to this point, but it still wasn't over.

I'd need a few weeks from surgery to begin radiotherapy as they needed time for the wound to heal. Meanwhile my scans had shown something in the chest area, but the doctors were sure it was something called sarcoidosis, some inflammatory condition and was nothing to worry about and preparations were made for those two treatments.

The third surgery was similar to the first, again I felt nauseous and groggy from the anaesthesia. I had gone from the patient who wanted little intervention to a patient that was having more surgeries than usual.

THIRTY-EIGHT

A Decade Later and Stage 4

After my surgery my doctor called me into the office, it was the original doctor I had seen on my first consultation. He cut to the chase.

"We've had the results back from the bronchoscopy biopsy and it looks like it is cancer."

He peered down his glasses. "We thought it wasn't, as it didn't seem like it was, but the biopsy has shown it's the same cancer that we found in the breast which has spread to the mediastinal lymph nodes. Ani, it is now considered to be Stage 4."

It was now a decade after the wave that changed my life.

2014.

Ten full years since I had emerged alive – and again I was facing death and having to fight for my life.

Shock stunned me into speechlessness, my mouth gaped like a goldfish, the world around me began spinning uncontrollably dancing. My worst cancer nightmare started to come true. I really was going to die. I wouldn't beat this after all and I began to wonder how long I had left.

"But, but you said it was sarcoidosis?' I replied, willing it to not be true.

"We thought it was, but the biopsy shows it's definitely cancer."

"So, what will you do? Will you take it out? Can you do surgery there?"

"We can't do surgery as it is so close to the heart and lungs."

"What about radiotherapy? I've just started so maybe you can add it to that?"

"Again, it's too close to the heart and lungs for us to do radiotherapy. We could irreparably damage those organs."

"What are you saying? There's nothing you can do?" Blind panic began to take over as thousands of unhelpful thoughts crowded my mind.

"We do have some other treatment options we would like to try first. It's a hormone medication called Zoladex. An injection you would take subcutaneously in the abdomen monthly. Zoladex works by stopping the ovarian function and the production of oestrogen. It would help to put you into an early chemically induced menopause."

He paused for a moment and looked at me kindly before continuing.

"We've had some very good results with the Zoladex, and it has been found to be an effective treatment for patients like you."

"When would I start?"

"I'll draw up the prescription for you and we'll make an appointment for you this afternoon downstairs for the nurses to administer it to you."

"I suppose there will be no kids now then?" I tearfully asked him.

"No, I'm sorry the zoladex would prevent you from being able to conceive."

Another loss of something I would never have.

The rest was a blur as arrangements were made to get me this new prescription and medication.

The nurses assured me that while it was technically S4 it really wasn't that bad as it hadn't spread to other parts of the body only to the mediastinal lymph nodes which are still kind of localised lymph nodes, this helped a little.

Finally, I left the hospital and couldn't get hold of Andrea in Amsterdam so frantically called Xan up in Scotland.

"I've got Stage 4!" I blurted out amongst heaving sobs.

"What?"

"The cancer it's stage 4, it's spread."

"What do you mean?" Xan replied.

"It's in my mediastinal lymph nodes. They're the lymph nodes around the chest."

"I thought they didn't think that was anything?"

"I know they made a mistake."

"What can you do? Can they do surgery?"

"No, it's too close to the heart and lungs they said! They are trying me on a new medication I must take monthly. Xan what am I going to do?"

PART III
Healing – Universal Lessons for All

THIRTY-NINE

Lesson 1: How Our Thoughts Shape Our Reality

I tried to take it all in but couldn't. I felt like I was being punished but for what? Had I really been so bad as to deserve all this? Surely not, I would wander back through the recesses of my mind trying to pick something that could have led to this final diagnosis.

The rest of the appointment was a muddle, shock kicking in once more.

That night I lay on the couch in the dark. My mind spinning with thoughts, I would finally have my reckoning. Meet my maker, and it will be over. The fear of death jangled all around me.

It dawned on me that all those years of depression had probably not been the greatest of signals to my body. Secretly wishing to be done with life had after all manifested in a life threatening disease. Had I unwittingly been the creator of my present day circumstances and my illness? Had one of my healers not already said to me she was getting a message that I didn't really want to be here and I needed to say yes to life?

Reading books that highlighted the mind, body, soul connection as well as my own lived experience made me understand the power that thoughts can have on our bio chemistry.

Thoughts beget our emotions and feelings, which when filtered through our *perspective*, in turn create our own reality and experience of life. Two people may get the same cancer diagnosis but will filter their experience or *reactions* through their own lens based on past life experiences, beliefs and evidence their brain finds, creating completely different realities. So if we master our thoughts and which ones we give our attention to as where your attention goes our energy flows, can we really master life?

I realised that if I had managed to create the life threatening illness through the persistent and negative thoughts of wanting to die I'd had for decades then what's to say I couldn't heal myself too? But I dismissed this thought for now as I was still in survival mode, in my primitive survival brain where fear ruled. Even though this semblance of hope cut through the darkness I was still dealing with a very real existential threat to me as a human.

The following morning I turned to Andrea.

"I need to go somewhere to ground myself, I can't manage all this, I am spinning out of control. Maybe we could go on holiday?" I ventured nervously biting my nails once more.

"Rather than going on holiday, why don't we go to this ashram in Wales? I have been following it for some time, the Swami there seems good and they have a good lineage and seem to be a serious ashram. It will help to be in a spiritual place rather than just a holiday."

"Great idea!" We drove straight down that day and the next morning woke up in the ashram. I pulled on my yoga clothes and headed to the hall and sat down and meditated. Later I got an audience and time to speak with the Swami.

Surrender and Letting Go

I told him my entire story.

"Maybe you need to surrender and accept all that has befallen you," he said simply.

"Perhaps now is the time to let universal consciousness / God do its thing. You know that they say what doesn't kill you makes you stronger so take this as that.

Sometimes these things come to us as messages so listen to what those messages are. We run courses here on accepting death as it is the one thing that is inevitable as soon as we are born. This is your opportunity to make peace with yours."

His words cracked open a light for me. It took the controlling fight out of my sails. The fight I had been fighting since Boxing Day 2004.

Acceptance

I had tried to control my diagnosis and my healing. I had tried to control my entire life. But now was the time to accept and reflect, to see the gifts in this challenge and what

I needed to remember and grow from to help me expand into what I was truly here for.

I couldn't control the external but I certainly could control my reactions and responses to what was happening. I was in charge of what thoughts I gave my attention to. I was in control of choosing life or staying miserable. I was responsible for choosing joy, love, and gratitude instead of finding imperfections with everything. All of that was in my control. If I accepted that all that had come to me had come for a specific reason from my soul to aid me in this life then there was nothing to fight against, merely to accept.

Trust

Finally I allowed myself to stop trying to control through fear and give in to trust. Have faith that everything that had happened till now was for a reason. I may not be able to understand that reason right now but with hindsight I would.

Trust—something I had never had a great relationship with—was now something I needed to surrender to and cultivate. Could I really trust all that life had dealt me? It seemed hard to see that this really had been for my benefit, but if kept remembering that we are spiritual beings having a human experience well I had been 'lucky' enough to be afforded a brief glimpse into the afterworld and the fullness of that knowledge and experience would serve me and others as time went on.

Go with the Flow

As I embraced trust, I realised there was another lesson waiting for me: learning to go with the flow. I was very good at being in charge or giving to others but I was not great at surfing the wave of life, allowing myself to go with the flow and / or receiving, until Andrea. Now would be the time to cultivate that, to recognise that all was as it was meant to be.

I had been sent Andrea at the most opportune time in my life, a true soul connection and spiritual being, one of the kindest, most non-judgmental people in a human form I had ever met. This wasn't a coincidence. He did after all share the same birthday as my dad who had passed away just after my cancer diagnosis and the realisation that this was all part of a greater plan dawned on me not for the first time.

When we truly allow ourselves this gift of going with the flow we create a more harmonious relationship with ourselves, others and universal forces at play. There's no need to fight—because with trust, surrender, and acceptance, there's nothing left to fight against.

FORTY

Lesson 2: Death is not the end, merely a transition to another dimension

As I dived into these newfound beliefs and concepts, my discussions with the Swami went deeper, we discussed confronting the fear of death and how to accept it as simply another transition. As someone who had already experienced near death, dying for a few seconds or minutes I knew deep down inside that death was NOT the end, our consciousness/spirit remains, our physical bodies are not real and the realisation that nothing and noone can truly hurt you on Earth because we are not the body resurfaced.

I had buried those memories but now they would serve me. My intuition had known that I didn't want to die in the hut, it had also known the tsunami was my near death experience and it also knew that cancer would be a 5 year journey but then I would be fine.

However I had let my primitive, survival brain that feeds and is ruled by fear to override my intuition and my deep consciousness that we all have. The evidence that I already had, that death is not the end and a mere transition and slowly the thriving part of my brain started to become stronger.

Fear and its Limits

They say that until you have made your peace with death, you never truly live, as the fear of dying hinders your ability to live. How many times do we stop ourselves from doing things because we fear the outcome? It doesn't even need to be a real, life-threatening danger, like public speaking, (one of the biggest fears we have) but our brains perceive it as one. This constant state of fear limits us, creating barriers that prevent us from experiencing life in its fullness.

I believed that when the soul has come here to do what it needs to do it passes on but we never truly die, we are eternal souls that simply transform matter.

If we never truly die and life is eternal as we are spiritual beings having a human experience, then surely there is nothing to fear in the first place?

Finding Peace

The days I spent here and in subsequent spiritual retreats allowed me to confront my mortality and make peace with my death whenever it would be. Life had already rewarded me with so many answers into the mysteries of life, I had simply chosen not to see them.

I had been doing this all my life I realised, but now was the catalyst for change, to transform and rise from the ashes like a phoenix. If I had created it so I could uncreate it and create something better instead. With this new found wisdom I set about creating a different reality.

FORTY-ONE

Lesson 3: You have the power of mastering your mind

When I first began meditating all the while back in 2010, when I had met the love of my life, like many, I struggled. Andrea had commented that I was the most fidgety person he had met in that yoga holiday place and I couldn't sit still for a minute. Like many, thoughts cascaded constantly into my mind, making it hard to meditate and clear your mind as so many had said you were supposed to do.

Andrea taught me that you don't have to clear your mind, simply observe the mind. This made it a lot easier. I still struggled to find gaps between the thoughts and often my mind would wander for many minutes before I would catch it and bring it back to the breath, or sensations in the body, sounds etc.

But a retreat at a Buddhist Thai temple where we were doing a 10 day Vipassana course in 2012 made me realise how much my thought field was consumed by thoughts of death and dying. It was my every other thought. I'd realised then that if I didn't get control of my mind, it would control me and so I started the long and often difficult road to mastering my mind.

I signed up for a year-long meditation course at the ashram in Wales. This would involve going back there one weekend every month to meditate and dive into a more spiritual life.

These weekends started to become a lifeline for me allowing me to deepen my practice and get quiet. They also allowed me to keep the connection to the Swami and the ashram both of which had been so instrumental in my coping with this all.

Following that I attended multiple 10 day silent vipassana retreats where you were supposed to meditate for 10 hours a day and sit in silence with no phones, or technology at all.

These Vipassana meditations were when my practice developed from trying to sit still and observe for a few minutes at a time and then jump up due to lack of concentration and uneasiness to actually having moments of peace in between the thoughts. Not just peace though but all the things buried deep beneath the surface like the trauma of the tsunami.

One morning at the retreat, I woke up with severe tonsillitis and I hatched a plan to leave. I was fed up with meditating for 10 hours a day and bored out of my mind–this gave me the perfect excuse to leave. But then I had a conversation with my mind/ego and decided to apply the practice they were teaching: non-reaction and observation. Despite waking up at 3:00 a.m. with a fever and white spots on my tonsils the size of golf balls, by 10:00 a.m., my fever had subsided. By 11:30 a.m. (lunchtime), my tonsils had returned to normal size, and by 3:00 p.m., all the spots had disappeared.

It was after this that I realised how strong the power of the mind could be and battened down the hatches to meditate properly for the rest of the course. In doing so, I chased balls of anxiety all around my body and felt in a state of terror and panic much of which seemed to be some of the trauma of the tsunami coming out.

I joked to myself that I would need to do about 10-20 of these to be a normal person, but it was after leaving this retreat that I really noticed my life changed. I became much calmer, my monthly hormonal explosive fights with Andrea diminished, my relationship with food changed and I comfort ate less. I was much less reactive and felt more peace and calm in my life. I wrote a blog about the 10 days that changed my life and sure enough that's how it felt.

Ease and Flow

I had saved the date of our marriage as I was about to go to my first one of these Vipassana's and we were to be married a month later. When I left the meditation centre after 11 days, I felt in ease and flow perhaps for the first time in my life and everything regarding my wedding was a breeze.

Friends rallied to get everything done, cakes were ordered by my best woman, my master of ceremony altered my dress. A close friend with design experience made my invites and other friends offered to host the reception. **Never** had things gone so smoothly before. It was a beautiful day filled with love and I was overwhelmed with love and gratitude for all my amazing and wonderful friends.

After this meditation course I was so enamoured with the results I did indeed go back multiple times, every 3 months to begin with until the pandemic struck. Making it to the 10-20 retreats I had previously joked about needing to do. Each one making significant changes to my health, peace of mind and joy.

Living in the NOW!

With meditation, I learnt to stay in the present moment and it was an art form I needed to master to deal with my diagnosis otherwise I would drive myself mad with the unknown and useless thoughts of when I will die.

The past holds us captive with the stories we tell ourselves of how our parents wronged us or how a traumatic experience stays with us. It is true the body stores these emotions but only if they are not released. The past doesn't actually exist anymore and the future is unknown. All that we truly have is the present moment which is a gift and is either seized upon and experienced or wasted and gone again.

How many of us spend our time ruminating over the mistakes we made in the past or worry about an uncertain future? Meanwhile we may never wake up tomorrow so all that worry would have been for nothing. Quite literally wasting your mental energy.

I gave up my dreams of having children. The universe had other plans for me. There was a reason why I had gone through as many challenges as I had I mused to myself, once again I didn't know what they were right now but they would become clearer as time went on.

With all these realisations and awareness I continued buoyed by my intuition that had stayed true to me all these years.

My Second Miracle

Three months later I went in for my next scan.

I sat there anxiously in the waiting room anticipating the results from my scan as the fear naturally crept in again. Finally, the doctor came in and after the usual small talk launched right in.

"Well, we have great news. There is NO EVIDENCE OF DISEASE from the scans. The lymph nodes have shrunk and aren't big enough for us to measure. It looks like whatever you are doing is working. We're very happy with the results so quickly, we're not sure we've seen such a spontaneous remission of the disease."

I looked at the doctor stunned but also wondrous.

"Really?" My primitive, survival brain answered doubting again . "But how come it vanished like that?"

"We're not sure, as I said we haven't seen something like this before, maybe you responded to the medication although it's quite early for that but perhaps all the other things you have been doing have helped also."

Perhaps all my work and realisations had paid off after all I thought to myself? Further evidence and clarification that my intuition had been right again, it was exactly 5 years from my original diagnosis. Exactly 5 years when my intuition had told me this would be a 5 year ordeal but I would survive it.

Andrea and I went out to celebrate that night.

How Stage 4 was Another Blessing in Disguise

The new medication they had me on ended up being another blessing in disguise. Whereas before I had been on a rollercoaster of hormones and spent half my life with premenstrual stress, feeling like Dr. Jekyll and Mr. Hyde now my rollercoaster is over. The Zoladex miraculously gave me the peace and quality of life I had been missing all these decades!

Suddenly I was only at the mercy of my hormones once every 2-3 months instead of every two weeks. This significantly improved so many aspects of my life.

My relationship with Andrea which had endured so much stress right from the onset, cancer diagnoses, death of my dad and my subsequent 5-year battle significantly improved. I felt an ongoing sense of peace and calm that had previously been only fleeting. I was no longer hampered by managing my hormonal ups and down and could now finally settle into who I really was.

Nothing had been as liberating as this. Now I understood why I had to go to Stage 4 before healing—this was the solution I had been searching for. Realising that most of my bad moods and survival brain/saboteur hijacking were the result of my errant hormones was a game changer. I no longer berated myself for the decisions I had made, as all of it had led me to this point: a quality of life that had been missing in my 40-plus years so far.

FORTY-TWO

Lesson 4: We All Have a Greater Purpose

Now what?

Exactly ten years on from the tsunami I had been diagnosed with and gone into remission from Stage 4 breast cancer.

I was no longer fighting for survival and my basic human needs of health and safety. Now I turned my attention to the rest of my life that I had neglected.

A bigger sense of purpose took the stage once again. I was still searching for meaning, the existential questions of why are we here, what is my purpose or destiny? How do I fulfil that?

I had taken these past five years to focus on my health but now I felt energised and well enough to revisit that. It wasn't important to just work but to fulfil this sense of meaning, fulfilment, something for the greater good, to serve and help others, just like I had in the aftermath of the tsunami.

Around the same time people naturally started gravitating to me to discuss their problems and ask for advice on various things happening in their life. They knew of what I had overcome and felt inspired. I had changed and a new found calmness became a magnet. It gave them hope that they too could get through their own difficulties and change for the better.

One day a member of my extended family and friends reached out to me and asked if I could help their family member. This person had been struggling with some personal challenges for a while and they didn't know how to help them. They asked if I could reach out to them to help.

I gladly did so, helping others helps yourself and it felt great to be of some use in life again. I had already completed qualifications and accreditations in Yoga Teaching, Yoga Therapy, Meditation, Mindfulness, Ayurveda, Hypnotherapy, Acupuncture, EFT, Reiki and NLP by now. Each of these qualifications deepened my knowledge and understanding of our psychology, and spiritual nature.

"Have you spoken to your therapist about these issues?" I asked this person.

"No, to be honest Ani I have found our discussions to have been more helpful than the therapists."

And it was then I had my lightbulb moment that perhaps everything I had gone through meant I had a gift on how to help others.

This person became my first coachee and I practised what I'd learnt on my coach training as well as all the other topics I already knew about.

Asking questions was second nature to a former journalist and now with intuition, a lot of formal learning and other skills and knowledge it was the perfect fit. I had always toyed with becoming a therapist or hypnotherapist but what put me off therapy was someone coming and talking about the same thing over and over, not because I didn't want to listen or sympathise but because I knew I would find it incredibly frustrating to see someone not moving forward.

But a blend of coaching and mentoring alongside all the other healing modalities was the perfect mix of moving people forward and getting them to shed the limits we put on ourselves to live their big, bold, beautiful lives.

My Eastern philosophical roots always brought me back to the point though that much of the self-development world focuses on being your 'best self'. But my philosophy is that we already were our 'best selves'; we just needed to *see* it and discard the noise of the false thoughts that ran around our brains.

Resilience

My journey, from childhood to tsunami, then cancer had been instrumental in shaping who I am now. It shows that no matter how tough things get, we all have the ability to overcome and grow. I'm not the first and certainly not the last.

I know my childhood and difficult relationship with my dad was the foundation of the core strengths I'd rely on in the tsunami. I wouldn't have had the capability that I did then to take on the role I did without having had the difficult upbringing I had.

Forgiveness

I worked hard on forgiving my parents for being the imperfect beings that they were and I ended up not only forgiving them, but thanking them for making me the strong person I turned into.

I forgave people that had 'wronged' me in the past and melted resentment and anger with love, compassion and forgiveness instead. I felt like the iceberg inside was melting, being replaced.

Compassion and Empathy

I was more empathetic and less judgmental. We are energetic beings, if one person is angry, the other person's neurons will automatically start mirroring theirs. If you are calm, compassionate and loving, that energy is also felt by others and you then become a magnet attracting that same energy back.

We can all feel when a person walks into a room and is angry or depressed and in that same way we feel when someone is happy and joyful we are drawn to them.

My path had opened my heart and I was more compassionate, this allowed me to connect with others more deeply.

Duality

Andrea and I would have endless discussions about light and darkness and how they were actually codependent; one couldn't exist without the other. In the west, we tend to demonise the darker side.

Eastern philosophies were more accepting of the duality of nature, with Hindu mythology talking of the Gods of Creation, Destruction and Maintenance. In the main religions it was always the devil vs God the struggle between good and evil, rather than perhaps understanding that we all have those elements within us, light and darkness and accepting them both with love and compassion for ourselves is the key.

Gratitude

I felt an increasing sense and state of gratitude as life progressed, despite the extreme hardships and challenges that I had to overcome, deep inside I knew they were all part of my soul's larger plan. The wisdom I had gleaned from everything I had gone through, I looked at with gratitude.

I no longer believed I was being punished by a ruthless God that exists in the sky rather that my soul had chosen my journey to create awakening in me and open my eyes to the reality of all I had come to know. I gave deep thanks for all I had gone through and realised all the pain had a pay off in the end.

Every Challenge is an Opportunity for Growth

I often think the universe has a plan for us and even if we can't see what that is from our perspective when we look back, we can see the opportunities and gifts that come our way through the challenges we have to overcome. We may not always understand why and where things come from but now every decision I had made was vindicated, even the ones delaying my treatment. As it had turned out into a better outcome that had surpassed anything I felt at the time.

I had cultivated acceptance, nonreaction to external stimuli, going with the flow and trusting the process of life and myself.

In Your Darkest Hour, You Find Your Greatest Strengths

I realised that it took me plunging to the depths of the darkness to find my greatest strength. All the challenges I had faced in my life so far had helped me be exactly the person I am today.

Without any one of those experiences I would be a different person. I know I probably wouldn't be able to help others the way I can now. Transmuting that darkness back into light and using that gift to shine a torch for others going through their own challenges is what I genuinely believe I went through all of this for. It gives me understanding and meaning to what I went through and fulfils the purpose I had always searched for.

What You Resist Persists

However you don't need to go through all of what I did to traverse life happily and in flow. I refused to listen to the signs, to my soul gently tapping me to say hey, "You're not on the right path." Turned into ginormous messages from the universe and my soul giving me sharp shocks to pivot. Because what you resist persists.

If you refuse to learn the lesson the first time you'll keep getting the same message in a different form. I think my soul got tired of giving me short sharp near death experiences and eventually turned to cancer to give me more time to make the changes I had too. That time I listened.

A Never Ending Journey

Once you've found your purpose and discovered what works in your life, it doesn't mean the journey is complete. The work isn't done; the journey continues and the tug between the ego mind / fear / survival brain and your thriving brain /consciousness continues and there may be times where you feel you are going three steps forward and two steps backwards, but you are always improving incrementally.

Meaning in what We Face

In the heightened days after that wave changed our lives, I had a strong sense of needing to make my life meaningful and purpose driven, whilst I didn't know back then what that would look like I knew it would become clearer as time passed.

I didn't get the life lesson the tsunami tried to teach me for a very long time. I spent a decade asking why I didn't die.

Why me?

It drove me into other flirtations with death.

It led me to my Stage 4 cancer diagnosis.

Was this all so life had to throw another curve ball at me to see if this next challenge would finally change the path of my life?

Unconditional Love for Ourselves

I realised the biggest truth of all is that our own self compassion, forgiveness, self-love and acceptance of ALL parts of ourselves is what will bring us the most peace, fulfilment and growth. That includes the shadow side and self-sabotaging archetypes we have. For if we do NOT accept and love those too we are rejecting parts of ourselves and this is not healthy for our mind, body and soul. Rather we fragment ourselves and deny and reject those sections which we may not like, creating not just world separation but separation within.

This universal truth I know is one of the hardest to truly implement. How to stop yourself berating yourself when you make a mistake, get angry, or frustrated with others, or even yell or worse lash out. How do you prevent yourself from rejecting those parts and STILL love yourself and forgive yourself for being imperfect? We just have to keep working on being kind, gentle and loving with ourselves.

The kinder, more loving and gentle we are with ourselves, the more we are also like that with others. Isn't that a great thing? Wouldn't you like to see more universal love, tolerance, kindness, peace and forgiveness in the world?

Embody the Change You Want to See

As Gandhi said, be the change you want to see in the world. Shifting our own consciousness has a knock on effect to those around us thereby creating a wave of positive change in the world. If we want to live in a world of peace, harmony, joy and love we must be the model of those qualities.

We are bigger and better than that and together we can make the world a better place, we just need to believe it. When I was younger I wanted to change the world. As I have matured I realise that we must *be* the change we want to see in the world. We must be the beacon of love, tolerance, forgiveness, empathy, kindness and understanding. When we can be those things we help shift universal consciousness for the better.

My Present Day – Content and Fulfilled

These days, rather than depression and anxiety, I wake up with a spring in my step full of the joys of life and love eager to start my day and live fully.

I am content, I'm relaxed and feel happy and at peace. I'm excited about the future, I have great friends, family, an amazing husband, a calling that I love, and my health has recovered.

I'm the happiest I've ever been in my life in a contented and fulfilled sense. I know that I am ready to share my story to help others know that there is light at the end of the tunnel, the journey may be rocky but if you persist and notice the signs and act on them life can be and is a glorious existence.

This doesn't mean I am immune to other challenging events in my life but now I have the tools, techniques, resources, faith, trust and hope to know that I can and will overcome them triumphantly and when it's my time I'll pass to the other side. A positive mental attitude helps with overcoming anything that life throws in your path. Mental fitness is my new superpower which I wield for the benefit of others.

Life is Happening For Us

I believe life is happening *for us* and through us not *to* us. How much more empowering is it to think like that rather than to feel victimised by what's happening to us? What if everything was being done with your soul's permission? Rather than just happening to us haphazardly?

Perfection Doesn't Exist

Don't get me wrong Pete Paranoia is still there, but his voice is quieter and I am able to get out of his negativity within minutes or hours rather than months or years as it was in the past. I still experience days where things are a struggle, but where I spent 10% of my time experiencing joy and the rest feeling stressed, angry or anxious. I have flipped this around and now experience positive emotions 80%-90% of the time and negative ones 10%-20% of the time. I have to remind my perfectionist streak that perfectionism doesn't exist and to live by the 80/20 rule.

My transformation wasn't an overnight sensation. Because I didn't know *how*. It took years of hard work and dedication to get to where I am now because of everything I had to process and no doubt there are still layers of further work to do. It's a cycle that goes on throughout life. I go on to share the how with you so that you too can transform your life for the better also.

I do believe that what we think today has a bearing on our future reality, but this still won't prevent death, grief and loss. Once we realise these emotions sit side by side with life and joy and attempt to understand and accept this basic dual law of nature then we can sit in those uncomfortable feelings just as well as we can in the comfortable ones. Accept them and not reject them.

Round Up

Sri and I are closer than ever. Luke, Sri's tsunami baby, is now a big strong, strapping man with a penchant for acting and singing. Nate and I are also still in touch and close after all these years. Trauma bonds that last.

I'm still in touch with Stefhan and Anneli who separated after the tsunami and are now both married to their respective partners with kids. Andrea and I are stronger than ever.

Mission

And I finally found my purpose and mission in life that I spoke to Oprah about.

To create a conscious community and positively transform the lives of over 250,000 to create a ripple effect of meaningful change across the world and help people live their lives with joy, peace and love in honour of those who died in the '04 tsunami.

I hope this book helps you recognize that you too can overcome any challenge you face, that challenges are simply opportunities for growth, and that, like me, you are stronger than you can ever imagine. There is a hero within us all. I am just an ordinary person like you who had extraordinary challenges I was faced with. If I have been able to transform all of those things into something positive, know that you too can do the same.

When will you start to be your true, authentic, shining self and be the hero of your story?

Epilogue

I began writing this book back in 2017 and I noticed how much I have changed not just since I started writing it but from who I was twenty years ago when the tsunami struck. What started as an idea turned into a deeply personal and detailed account of some of the darkest moments in my life. The struggles I faced as a young thirty year old trying to find my way in the world and desperately seeking the meaning of life and purpose. I grew up with a rough childhood which created perfectionism, overachieving and controlling behaviours. I battled with an inner critic so strong I felt I was worthless, lacked confidence and constantly criticised myself. I cowered and whimpered under its power.

This critic was also there with others, harsh on those around me, with high expectations and impossible standards set for all. It took me years to realise that the judgement of myself and others was a simple reflection of my inner world spilling out into the outer one.

These traits I developed in my formative years were the cause of much of my misery as an adult. Once I hit my career goal in my early 20s of becoming a Broadcast Journalist at the BBC, I questioned the meaning of life, and wondered is that all there is? This idea that this was all there is to life prompted a very real existential crisis that had me in a web of darkness for many years.

I noticed how much I changed from the person I once was to the person I am today. We all change to some extent but to what level is determined by how much you want to and how to adapt to the circumstances around you.

As I studied more on neuroscience and psychology, I learnt that we all have what's called a negativity bias. The negativity bias is where we remember the one thing that didn't go right in our week and or overly focus on painful and negative emotions rather than positive ones. It explains why we tend to remember the negative comments rather than the compliments and react more strongly to negative experiences than to positive ones.

It makes sense as our ancestors needed to identify the things that were dangerous to our survival rather than focus on the beautiful harmless things around us. Who cared about the harmless yet beautiful butterfly when there were poisonous snakes and sabre tooth tigers to contend with?

This negativity bias that is hardwired into our survival brains made me focus on the bad parts of my childhood and all the wrongs that had happened to me in my life rather than seeing the beauty and love that surrounded me. It's what keeps people in a perpetual state of moaning or complaining and seeing fault with themselves, others or others ideas.

This was a huge relief when I learnt about it — I wasn't mad, bad or sad I was just behaving how humans are predisposed to doing so.

There are two main hemispheres of the brain, let's call one surviving and the other thriving.

On one side, there's the surviving or the lizard brain, which is driven by fear, survival instincts, and the ego, or sense of self. This part of the brain is connected to the body's sympathetic nervous system, which is responsible for the fight-or-flight response.

On the other side, there's the thriving or "wizard" brain. This part is linked to the parasympathetic nervous system, which promotes relaxation and is associated with positive emotions and growth.

Now we need both parts of the brain to survive. They are complementary to one another, but we don't always want the lizard brain to dominate, as it would lead us to live in constant fear of what might go wrong. Our lizard brain isn't concerned with whether you have a fulfilling life or not, which is why we need to balance the two.

Mental fitness helps us shift from our primitive, fear-driven survival brain into our greater consciousness, or thriving brain—this is what I help myself and others do now. When we allow the lizard brain to take control, we descend into fear-based behaviours like jingoism, racism, and sexism, forgetting that we are all part of one divine consciousness. This division keeps us disconnected from our true selves and each other.

This disconnect also fuels our self-sabotaging voices, which originate in our early years as natural coping mechanisms designed to protect us. However, as we let the survival brain take over, these voices linger into adulthood, continuing to hold us back. Unless we become aware of them and consciously work to weed them out, they keep us playing small, focused on survival rather than growth.

These voices, though protective, are not aligned with our highest purpose or our authentic, soulful selves.

There are many of these archetypes of self-sabotaging voices, and you may recognise some of them in yourself. Maybe you're an overachiever, a perfectionist, or feel the need to control everything. Perhaps you're a people pleaser or tend to think, "Why me?"— that's the Victim archetype. Do you procrastinate, avoid tasks, or shy away from conflict? These are all examples of self-sabotaging behaviours, often personified as the Controller, Overachiever, Avoider, People Pleaser, Victim, and Perfectionist. Among them, the loudest voice or the 'Master Saboteur' is the Judge, which critiques ourselves, others, and our circumstances.

Did you know that all of our negative emotions come from one of our saboteur archetypes? They are the cause of all of our unhappiness, guilt, frustration, suffering and sadness.

But once you understand the basic principles of our psychology and neuroscience you can direct your life how you would like to. Just be aware of the procrastination monsters or the fear of living your true light that will hamper you along the way. Why do you think it took me seven years to finish writing this book?

Mental Fitness / Emotional Resilience

Mental fitness is our ability to handle life's challenges with a positive rather than a negative mindset. It involves developing a mindset that allows us to manage stress, overcome obstacles, and approach problems with a constructive outlook. Essentially, mental fitness equips us to handle adversity without being overwhelmed by negativity or fear.

As I have mentioned, the survival brain has a tendency to dominate *unless* we intervene and do mental fitness exercises. Just as physical health requires 30 minutes of daily exercise, mental and emotional well-being demands 15 minutes of dedicated mental fitness practice. These exercises are crucial for shifting our brain from a fear-driven survival mode to a thriving state, where we approach life with greater resilience, clarity, and positivity. Without regular mental fitness practices, we risk falling back into survival mode, which fuels fear, anxiety, and a sense of separation based on race, religion, sex, culture, and other divides.

How-to and Tools and Techniques that Increase Mental fitness

There are a variety of things that can help you. We have the power to shift our awareness and our neuroplasticity and many activities can do that for us. Some of the most effective and powerful techniques to do this are meditation and mindfulness practices. There have been many research studies done now that highlight how Buddhist monks have whole regions of their brain activated which non meditators don't.

You can completely rewire your neural pathways in the brain so you too can shift from surviving to thriving with some simple exercises a day.

There are many forms of meditation or mindfulness practices and none are better or worse than others, more a case of personal preference. One of the easiest ones for anyone to start with is to observe the breath. Breathing in for a count of 4 and breathing out for a count of 8. This slow breathing technique is designed to activate the parasympathetic nervous system and activates you into your thriving brain.

Another one is super simple which is a 10-second focus on one sense, whether that's the breath, sound, visual, touch or taste. Refocus all your awareness just for 10 seconds on one of these aspects and it automatically helps you engage the thriving part of your brain. If you were to do this regularly throughout the day, you would ensure that you are operating through your thriving brain and you will have more focus, productivity, performance, clarity, empathy and emotional intelligence throughout the day. If you are an executive or leader, you will be able to do more work in less time whilst increasing your self-care and wellbeing.

Imagine redirecting all of our negative thought energy, which is spent in worrying, into creating energy instead? How much more could you achieve in your life if you were able to do that? Ask yourself: a) How much of your thought energy are you aware of? b) How much are you in charge of? c) How much is directed towards positive thoughts versus negative ones? If the answer is less than 75%, you are likely operating in your survival brain more often than not. We need our mental fitness score to be at least 75% to counteract the 3-to-1 negativity bias.

These are the techniques I used that helped me shift my own plasticity from being in a constant stressed, survival mode to now thriving and it is my passion to share that with others as for many years I had no idea as to *how* to change.

I serve others and help them to shed their negativity and self-sabotaging thoughts and behaviours and shine a light of hope so that they too can align to their true self so they can live their purpose and find joy, freedom and meaning in their lives.

I understood and learnt about the negativity bias and how our primitive, survival brain makes us inherently prone to seeing all the bad things in life. I also discovered how we can shift our neuroplasticity through regular meditation, mindfulness and gratitude practice.

As a Transformation Coach and Mentor, I am dedicated to helping people unlock their full potential. Whether you're a CEO, doctor, high performer, leader or executive, my mission is to support you on your journey to becoming the best version of yourself. The people I work with come from all walks of life, but they share one thing in common: the desire for meaningful, lasting change.

My work is not just a career—it's a calling. I am deeply honoured to witness the profound transformations in my clients' lives, and I feel incredibly grateful to be part of their journey.

Through my keynote speaking engagements, media appearances, and podcast, (Bits of Wisdom) I share the lessons I've learned to empower and serve others. I want you to know that no matter what challenges you face, you too can live a bold, authentic, and fulfilling life. My goal is to reach as many people as possible, empowering them to overcome their obstacles and step into their greatness.

In addition to one-on-one and group coaching, I offer corporate training on mental fitness, helping thousands of people achieve breakthroughs that not only transform their lives but also positively impact those around them.

One Salesforce leader I worked with shared how my coaching helped her become a better leader, which in turn uplifted her entire team. It's moments like these that show the ripple effect of personal transformation—it goes beyond the individual, creating a wider impact on families, teams, and communities.

I've had the privilege of witnessing incredible outcomes, from a client naming her baby after me after a successful pregnancy journey, to another client finding love after 20 years of being single. These experiences reaffirm my belief in the power of growth, resilience, and transformation.

The wisdom I gained from surviving the tsunami and my battle with cancer has shaped everything I do today. My mission is to share that knowledge with you, so that you can achieve the transformation you're seeking—without having to go through the same struggles. Together, we can make sure that your challenges become the foundation for your greatest growth

It's why I wrote this book — fighting Pete Paranoia (my inner critic voice) all along the way, going against my fears of being judged and sharing some of the most intimate and terrifying parts of my life for all to see. But when you have a story such as mine and have managed to come out the other side I'd like to think it serves as a beacon of light and hope for others and those in the darkness.

If you have read this far, I would like to thank you for allowing me to share my story with you. I hope that you find inspiration and feel empowered, knowing that you too can overcome whatever challenges you face and live the beautiful life you were meant to live.

Remember, you CAN and WILL overcome your challenges. We are ALL so much stronger than we can ever imagine we could be. Shine as bright as you can, celebrate the hero within you, and use that power to transform the world for the better. Create a wave of positivity through universal love, rooted in unconditional self-love, embracing both the shadow and the light, and forgiveness for our spiritual beings having a human experience.

To join the movement go here www.ultimateresultsgroup.com

To connect with me you can email me at ani@ultimateresultsgroup.com, follow me on social media ani.naqvi instagram, Ani Naqvi on Linked in and Facebook. Listen to our podcast Bits of Wisdom on spotify and apple music and join my movement for transformation.

From me to you, with love and light.

The End

Acknowledgments

I want to acknowledge all the people and events that have led me to this path. Firstly, I'd like to acknowledge all the experiences I feel blessed to have had to bring me to where I am today.

I'd also like to acknowledge all the support from all the people who have helped me in various ways. These include all of my clients, teachers, and mentors. This list is by no means all of those who have touched my life but a simple attempt to acknowledge some of them. They include my parents, Birjees Naqvi and Masood Naqvi.

People who have helped me along the path, including Srianjali Gunasena, Nate Berkus, Swami Nischalanda, Becky Duffy, Sarah Bullen, Kate Emmerson, David Allison, Phil Cohen, Landi Jac, Neale Donald Walsch, Stephanie Larkin, and Mike Handcock, are just a few of them. Plus the thousands of clients who have taught me just as much as I have them.

I also want to acknowledge all my spiritual guides along the way, the sages and masters that have lived throughout time of the main religions and all the teachings from my Eastern philosophical roots, including the Vedas and Buddhist philosophies which both expanded my awareness ever more.

About the Author

Ani Naqvi is a London-born British Asian, married to her Italian husband, Andrea, and they adore living in and travelling to different parts of the world.

Her mission is to ignite a movement of positive change around the world by transforming the lives of over 250,000 people. Driven by remembrance and resolve, Ani channels the loss from the world's largest natural disaster of our lifetime into a purpose that transcends borders. Having survived when so many did not, she dedicates her efforts to honour those who died – transforming her survival into a legacy of hope, healing, and lasting impact.

Ani's story has been featured in major media outlets such as *The Oprah Winfrey Show*, *The Daily Telegraph*, *Channel 4*, *BBC News*, the *Metro*, *Daily Express*, and *Forbes*.

Ani began her career as a BBC Broadcast Journalist before moving into Program work and now works as a Transformation Coach & Mentor for senior executives who work for global brands. She is a corporate mental fitness trainer, inspirational speaker, and podcaster.

Her work has touched the lives of hundreds of CEOs, Executives, Leaders, Doctors/Lawyers and elite performers, empowering them to achieve greater success, performance, and productivity while simultaneously increasing well-being and ultimately reducing the risk of burnout.

Tsunami, The Wave that Saved My Life and Can Save Yours is Ani's debut memoir, chronicling her journey from the devastation of the tsunami to finding hope, strength, and purpose. Through this deeply personal narrative, Ani shares her own transformation and the life lessons she gained from overcoming adversity and how these experiences have shaped her mission to make a positive difference in the world.

In her spare time, Ani loves all things musical. She enjoys singing and has been taking voice lessons in preparation for joining a pop choir. She is also fond of dancing and does so whenever she can.

www.ingramcontent.com/pod-product-compliance
Lightning Source LLC
Chambersburg PA
CBHW072147070526
44585CB00015B/1035